NUREMBERG

Published by IWM, Lambeth Road, London SE1 6HZ
iwm.org.uk

ISBN 9781912423989

A catalogue record for this book is available from the British Library.
Printed and bound by Gomer
Colour reproduction by DL Imaging

EU Authorised Representative: EAS Europe – Mustamäe tee 50, 10621 Tallinn, Estonia, gpsr.requests@easproject.com

Front cover: IWM (HU 71699 / artistic rendition 2025)
Back cover: IWM (Art.IWM ART LD 5725)

NUREMBERG

James Bulgin & Toby Haggith

CONTENTS

36

CHAPTER ONE

Introduction

Prisoners at Bergen-Belsen sit by the wire fence dividing the various sections of the camp. They are eating their first meal after the liberation of the camp in April 1945.

The Nuremberg trial, officially known as the International Military Tribunal (IMT), was ambitious in its aims, scope and execution. It was not merely a war crimes trial, but a public reckoning into the criminality of the Nazi regime, carried out with reference to a new code book of international laws created especially for the trial, and with the authority to execute the convicted.

The trial was steeped in symbolism as much as in legal process. It sought to confront the poisonous legacy of the Nazis and their atrocities, dismantle the ideological foundations of the regime and lay the groundwork for a new international order. In the courtroom, arguments unfolded on both sides, not only over recent events, but also over decades of history, stretching back to the First World War and earlier.

The trial was modern in its technology, culture and legal practice. Its innovations and methods still resonate today. Yet much remains to be uncovered about the trial. Some records have only recently come to light and others – like the original film reels of the proceedings – still require restoration and greater accessibility. This book aims to draw the reader's attention to the rich collection of artworks, documents, films, photographs and recorded interviews relating to the IMT held in the collections of IWM.

Given the scale and significance of the trial, it is surprising how swiftly preparations for Nuremberg were put into motion. Joint work between the Allied powers, to draw up what became the Nuremberg Charter, did not start until 26 June. Yet discussions on how to bring German war criminals to justice had begun in 1940, as Allied governments debated how best to punish the Nazi state for its invasion of the countries of Europe. These conversations were fraught with disagreements between the Allies over the form that justice should take. It wasn't until the spring of 1945 that a consensus was reached.

It was likely no coincidence that President Harry S Truman's final decision to try the Nazi leadership took place on 17 April, just two days after the liberation of Bergen-Belsen. The scenes uncovered there – where 70,000 had died – were among some of the most shocking of a series of dreadful discoveries made by Allied forces as they advanced through Germany and Austria. These grim revelations hastened preparations for a trial. Echoing this development, the Psychological Warfare Division of Allied command commissioned an Anglo-American documentary film on the Nazi concentration camps. It was envisaged as a visual criminal investigation report prepared for a prosecutor, ready to be presented at a war crimes trial.

The Nuremberg trial was held in Germany under the authority of the Allied powers: the US, the Soviet Union, Britain and France. These tribunals formed the highest tier of a tripartite structure of trials designed to prosecute individuals across the full spectrum of the Nazi hierarchy, from senior Party officials and military leaders down to lower ranking Nazi functionaries and members of the armed forces. Backed by international agreement and shaped by months of negotiation, the trials were a united effort to establish the legal framework and practical mechanisms needed to hold the German perpetrators of the war accountable.

The IMT, also known as the Trial of the Major War Criminals, officially opened in Berlin on 18 October 1945, before moving to the Palace of Justice in Nuremberg from 20 November 1945 to 1 October 1946. In the dock sat 21 of the 24 men accused – figures who had occupied the highest ranks of the Nazi regime.

A view of the Palace of Justice in Nuremberg, where the IMT trial of war criminals was held.

The Route to the IMT

At the time, there was no standing international court to prosecute crimes of war, but a framework of laws and treaties did exist to regulate relations between nations and to impose limits on the offences committed on the battlefield. These agreements addressed the treatment of prisoners of war (POW) and the care of enemy wounded; they prohibited the use of weapons, such as expanding bullets and poison gas. They also sought to shield civilian populations from abuse and murder by warring armies.

In the aftermath of the First World War, the Treaty of Versailles had included provisions for an international tribunal to prosecute the German Kaiser for initiating conflict, along with 845 German military personnel accused of violating the laws and customs of war. Yet the tribunal was never established; the Kaiser was not prosecuted and only 45 German servicemen were indicted. In the end, few were held to account, and the widespread perception was that German war criminals had largely escaped justice.

The failure to bring German war criminals to justice after the First World War cast a long shadow over Allied thinking during the global conflict which followed a generation later. As reports of the atrocities mounted, and the scale and nature of the crimes being committed in German-occupied Europe far surpassed those of the First World War, the Allies began publicly to commit to bringing war criminals to justice. As early as April 1940, official statements were issued declaring their intention to pursue punishment – not only on moral grounds, but also as a deterrent to ongoing crimes being committed in German-occupied zones.[1]

In October 1941, President Franklin D Roosevelt and Prime Minister Winston Churchill, condemning the Nazis' murder of French hostages, warned that 'retribution' for such crimes would follow, with Churchill stating this was now among the 'major purposes of the war'.[2] These statements culminated in a United Nations (UN) declaration that was read aloud in parliament, on 17 December 1942, and broadcast globally from London in 23 languages. It condemned the Nazi extermination of Jewish people and warned those responsible that 'They reaffirm their solemn resolution to ensure that those responsible for these crimes shall not escape retribution…'.[3]

When questioned after this announcement, Foreign Secretary Anthony Eden said that 'it was the intention that all persons responsible, whether ringleaders or perpetrators, should be treated alike and brought to book'.[4] These declarations were often made in tandem with the governments-in-exile of occupied nations, such as Czechoslovakia, France and Poland, on whose lands these atrocities had been committed. The Allied warnings stressed retribution and punishment rather than justice. For much of the war, both the British and Americans favoured summary execution – locating war criminals and shooting them on the spot without trial – although there is no evidence to suggest this was actually instituted. This policy extended to the Nazi leaders as well as those committing the crimes on the ground. Churchill, in particular, viewed such actions as a necessary purge to restore peace and order in post-war Europe. He and other members of the British government were wary of a formal war crimes trial, fearing it might offer the Germans a platform to spout propaganda. They were also unsure of the legality of such a process.

The Moscow Declaration

The next major step in the development of war crimes justice came at the Moscow Conference in October 1943. It marked the first meeting of the foreign secretaries of the US, Great Britain and the Soviet Union, with the primary aim discussing how to shorten the war and shape the nature of the peace that would follow. The conference concluded with a powerfully worded joint Statement on Atrocities – the strongest warning issued yet to Nazi Germany. The declaration affirmed the Allies' resolve to pursue war criminals 'to the uttermost ends of the earth', and listed various examples of atrocities already committed by the German forces. The declaration was careful to include shades of culpability, implicating those who had 'taken a consenting part in the atrocities…'.[5]

Although the statement did not explicitly mention trials, it hinted for the first time at a formal legal process, suggesting that justice would be administered in court rather than

The Moscow Conference in session in October 1943.

summary executions. Yet this form of justice was not intended for all German war criminals. The declaration drew a clear distinction between perpetrators operating at a lower level, 'German officers and men and members of the Nazi party', and 'German criminals whose offences have no particular geographical location'[6] – a phrase widely understood to refer to Adolf Hitler and the senior Nazi leadership. To ensure accountability, the former group would be returned to the countries where their crimes had been committed, to be tried under local jurisdiction. This marked a significance departure from the First World War, where German war criminals were tried in German courts. This clause was controversial as it potentially allowed victims to judge their offenders, risking justice turning into vengeance, and commentators warned that such trials might be seen as acts of retribution by the victors. According to the declaration, the Nazi leadership would not be subject to a legal trial, instead they were to 'be punished by joint decision of the government of the Allies'.[7] As one British expert in international law, approvingly explained:

> No judicial method could affect a clear decision of the issue. The crime of which Hitler has been guilty SURPASES ANY TRIAL AND CONDEMNATION...and in view of the gravity of the charge it would unquestionably be WISE THAT THE PENALTY PRONOUNCED SHOULD BE DEATH.[8]

To reinforce their commitment to justice, the United Nations Commission for the Investigation of War Crimes was established in London on 20 October 1943. Its task was to compile lists of suspected war criminals and to determine how best to bring them to justice.

Even before the Commission's creation, the first war crimes trials had already begun. In July 1943,[9] the Soviets held proceedings in Krasnodar, the Soviet Union, followed by further trials in Kharkov, Kiev in 1944, and then Lublin in Poland in November and December 1944.[10] The British, too, held, or supported, war crimes trials in Italy following its liberation from German occupation. These early cases reflected the first category of thc Moscow Declaration, with the accused tried in the countries where the crimes had been committed.

By the autumn of 1944, a shift was underway in American policy. The initial preference for summary executions of Nazi leaders began to give way to the idea of formal war crimes trials. Within the War Department, there was growing favour for an international tribunal – a judicial process that would be considered a more legitimate method of justice but also serve as a safeguard against the resurgence of Nazism. It was seen as a more fitting response to the democratic values upheld by the Allies and aligned with the aspirations of the UN. There were also military concerns: simply executing war criminals without trial, as the Allies advanced, risked provoking reprisals against

Allied POW.

The proposed trial of the Nazi leadership was intended to address the full scope of the regime's criminality – not just the war crimes committed by Germany's armed forces. Pressured by the demands and grievances of refugees, Jewish groups and the exiled governments of occupied Europe, the Americans proposed convicting the Nazi leaders for pre-war crimes committed in Germany and Czechoslovakia, the unprovoked invasion of Europe and for the murder, extermination, deportation, imprisonment and other atrocities committed against large numbers of civilians in German-occupied Europe. To make such a broad range of charges possible, prosecutors introduced the blanket charge of conspiracy to cover all the above crimes. They also designated key Nazi governing bodies as criminal organisations, enabling the arrest and prosecution of individuals based solely on by their membership to a Nazi organisation. By January 1945, President Roosevelt had been persuaded that the leading Nazi war criminals should be tried. However, with the war continuing and other priorities pressing, a formal shift on Allied policy did not occur until after Roosevelt's death.

While American policy was transitioning, the British government was compiling lists of Nazi leaders to be executed after capture. When news of the American change in direction reached British officials, they argued firmly against it. The Lord Chancellor, Viscount Simon, proposed a compromise: he accepted the contentious classification of Nazi institutions as 'criminal organisations'[11] for the purpose of prosecuting the lower-level war criminals, but insisted on retaining the Moscow Declaration's policy for Hitler and the Nazi leaders. Under this model, the Allied governments would jointly decide on punishment, either execution or a lengthy imprisonment, without the need for a trial. Even this compromise proved a step too far for the British Cabinet, which rejected the idea of a trial of the Nazi leaders altogether.[12] However, on 17 April 1945, President Truman – a former judge – dismissed Britain's objections and confirmed that a trial of the Nazi leaders would go ahead. Britain's bargaining position was weakened further by the stance of other Allied powers. The Soviet Union, which had favoured show trials, came to support a full judicial process, recognising that it would bring legitimacy to the Soviet regime.[13] For Joseph Stalin, the issue was also personal and political: without a trial, he feared, he, Churchill and Roosevelt might be accused of executing Hitler and his entourage out of vengeance.[14] The French, too, made their preference clear: they favoured a trial. On 3 May 1945, the British government finally accepted that the argument had been lost.

Preparations for the Trial

The planning for the IMT took place during the London Conference, held from 26 June to 8 August 1945. It was led by US Attorney General Robert Jackson. The Americans pushed for a broad and ambitious trial – one that would break new ground in international law. They proposed a sweeping set of new charges, including conspiracy to plan and start a war, crimes against humanity and the classification of German state institutions – such as the Reich Cabinet and the military high command – as criminal organisations. These charges reflected their ambitions to punish Nazi Germany for its aggressive unprovoked war, to prosecute for crimes committed even before the invasion of Poland and to expand the reach of international law in the hope that the horrors of the Second World War would never be repeated.

The Americans envisioned a trial with as many as 100 to 150 defendants in the dock. The British, however, were more cautious. Concerned about how to secure successful convictions with new legal concepts, they pushed for a smaller trial, with fewer defendants and a focus on established war crimes.

By the time of the Conference, the British had become more amenable to the idea of a large-scale trial. With the new responsibilities of occupying Germany, they valued the legitimacy of a public legal process that would expose the full extent of the atrocities and criminality of the Nazi regime.[15] Yet despite this shift, concerns remained – particularly around the complexity of mounting a trial for which there was no clear precedent. Both the British and the French expressed reservations about some of the new charges proposed by the Americans – notably the crime of launching an aggressive war. They feared it would be regarded as an *ex post facto* – punishing

individuals for actions that had not been defined as crimes at the time they were committed. The British were also worried that accusing the Germans of illegal invasion of territories might invite uncomfortable comparisons with Britain's own imperialism. The other controversy was around the defining of Nazi state organisations as criminal.

To satisfy the leading powers, the Conference also had to amalgamate the laws of two different legal systems: Anglo-American and continental. Some consideration was even given to German legal practice from the Weimar era. The differences between the two systems were considerable. In the continental tradition, followed by the French and Soviets, judges play the central role, weighing the evidence and deciding the verdict. Lawyers have a much smaller role under this system, which contrasts to the Anglo-American model, where the adversarial process is driven by the lawyers and cross-examination is central. The French and the Soviets struggled to grasp the importance of lawyers in Anglo-American law, particularly the need for cross-examinations, and were unfamiliar with the charge of conspiracy, which was central to the Americans' strategy for prosecution.

Justice Robert Jackson at the Nuremberg trial.

The London Agreement

On 8 August 1945, the four Allied powers signed the London Agreement, establishing the IMT. Alongside it, they created the Charter of the Tribunal, which gave jurisdiction to try Major Axis criminals for crimes against peace, war crimes and crimes against humanity. They were united by Count One, an overarching charge of Conspiracy or Common Plan to commit each of these foregoing crimes. The Charter also indicted leading organisations of the Nazi regime as criminal organisations. This meant that individuals could be tried on the basis of their membership to these criminal bodies. Among those named were the *Sturmabteilung*, or the SA, the *Schutzstaffel* (SS), including the *Sicherheitsdienst* (SD) and the *Geheime Staatspolizei*, known as the *Gestapo*, or Secret State Police. Also listed were the Reich Cabinet, the leadership of the Nazi Party and the General Staff and High Command of the German Armed Forces.

As the Americans drove, funded, hosted and ultimately ran the trial, the proceedings were primarily rooted in Anglo-American law, but some aspects of continental law were incorporated:

The London Conference in session, preparing for the Nuremberg trial, c.July 1945.

- **In contrast to British legal practice, where even military tribunals typically involve a single judge, the IMT adopted the continental model of a multi-judge panel.** Four judges, one from each of the governing powers, presided over the trial and all were required to be present for the court to be quorate. Each judge also had an alternate. The judges were as follows: President Lord Justice Lawrence (UK); Justice Norman Birkett (UK); Francis Biddle (US); John J Parker (US); Professor Donnedieu de Vabres (France); Monsieur Robert Falco (France); Major-General of Jurisprudence I T Nikitchenko (the Soviet Union), and Lieutenant-Colonel A F Volchkov (the Soviet Union).

- **There was no jury.** In line with continental law, the judges determined both the guilt and sentencing of the defendants. A majority of three out of four was required for conviction, with the president – selected by the panel from among themselves before the trial – holding the casting vote in the event of a tie.

- **The preference for documentary evidence over oral testimony at the IMT reflected the continental system's influence.** Under Anglo-American law, witness testimony is often a prioritised source of evidence.[16]

- **The adversarial structure of the trial was distinctly Anglo-American.** Prosecution and defence lawyers presented their arguments in turn, arbitrated by a judge in allotted sections of the proceedings. This format was unfamiliar – and at times baffling – to the French and Soviet prosecutors and the German defence counsel.

A core but unstated aim of the trial was to conduct a thorough examination of the Nazi regime, regardless of how long it might take. Concerns had been raised about the potential length of the proceedings after the Belsen trial, which some felt had dragged on too long. Justice Jackson shared these concerns and introduced Articles 18(a) and 18(b) of the Charter to prevent the trial dragging on. During the trial, the judges often intervened to push the proceedings along. Still their overriding priority – and that of the prosecutors – was to ensure the case was examined thoroughly, even if that meant extending the length of the proceedings.

Fairness

One of the guiding principles of the trial was that it must be conducted fairly to prevent it being dismissed by the defeated nations, particularly Germany and Austria, as a kangaroo court, practising victors' justice. To guard against this, the Tribunal's Charter codified, in Clause IV, a Fair Trial for Defendants. Article 16 of the Charter laid out specific protections for the accused. All trial papers and the court proceedings were to be translated, and defendants were to be given prior access to the indictment and prosecution's evidence. They were also entitled to defend themselves or be represented by legal counsel. This stipulation was further reinforced in Article 23, which gave each defendant the right to choose their own lawyer. Article 29 prevented the Allied Control Council for Germany – the executive authority in post-war Germany – from increasing the severity of any sentence imposed by the Tribunal. Yet there were also limits to the Tribunal's generosity. Anticipating the defences that many of the accused were likely to offer, the Charter simply made them out of bounds. Article 7 stated that there would be no immunity for Heads of State or senior government officials. Article 8 went further and ruled that the excuse of 'just following orders' was not a valid defence at Nuremberg.

As the opening of the trial approached, there was hope that the proceedings would be swift – perhaps completed in as a few as 50 working days. Preparations had progressed smoothly, 'like clockwork',[17] according to Sir David Maxwell

Fyfe, and both the defence and prosecution were said to have their cases prepared. There was also an air of excitement about this ambitious trial, with its lofty aims, its translation into four languages and its broadcast to the world. On the opening day, Lord Justice Lawrence captured the gravity of the moment, calling it 'unique in the history of jurisprudence'.[18] Yet to many observers, its true significance didn't lie in its legal innovation, but in the promise it offered to humanity: 'The proof of the Nuremberg Trial will be in the verdict of the Judges on whom is cast the tremendous responsibility of establishing a precedent on which will depend the world's hope of realistically outlawing war.'[19]

·N·S·D·A·P·

CHAPTER TWO

Why Nuremberg?

Adolf Hitler addresses the assembled crowd at the 1935 Nuremberg Rally. The 'Nuremberg Laws' would be announced as part of the same event.

The final months of the Second World War saw a significant escalation in the Allied bombing campaign in Germany. British and American heavy bombers laid waste to vast swathes of major German cities, bolstered by total air supremacy and vastly superior output of planes and armaments. This intensification caused extraordinary levels of damage. The vicious urban fighting that followed consolidated this, destroying much of what was left. This devastation not only resulted in the deaths of countless people and the displacement of millions more, but by the end of the war, it also left much of the country's infrastructure in tatters.

For the teams charged with identifying a site for the post-war tribunal, this caused a problem. While it had always been their intention to hold the proceedings in Germany, finding somewhere that this was practically possible was another question entirely. Most of the country's major cities were in ruins and there were few obvious options for a major – and unprecedented – international trial.

The task of finding such a location was overseen by Robert Jackson – who was keen to take responsibility for all major decisions during these early stages. When Nuremberg was first proposed to him as an option, in characteristic fashion, he travelled there in person to assess its suitability. Though around 90 per cent of the city had been destroyed in a series of major raids during the war, its courthouse – the Palace of Justice – had miraculously survived, as had the prison besides it. Fortuitously 'The Grand', a sizeable hotel nearby, was also

largely intact, albeit with a gaping hole in one section.

The courthouse would need some modification but was in principle big enough to accommodate the Allies' plans. The prison offered suitable accommodation for the defendants as well as a space that could be used for executions, should the requirement arise. The hotel would meet the needs of the prosecutors and their growing support staff. The utilities that served all these facilities also remained largely functional, meaning that not only did the structures exist but that they were also usable.

In addition to these practical issues, Nuremberg's status as the figurative heart of the Third Reich added some extra appeal to its suitability for the trial. During the Holy Roman Empire it had been an important imperial city, and Hitler saw his party's presence there as evidence of the continuity between that period of history and his rule. In the early years of the Nazi regime, his propagandistic mass rallies in the city's newly-built assembly grounds – which spanned around 11 square kilometres – had developed a notorious status. At these annual gatherings hundreds of thousands of uniformed followers would stand in orderly formation in front of a huge platform from which their leader would address them.

Hitler's personal architect and later armaments minister, Albert Speer, lined the parade ground with 152 anti-aircraft searchlights, the beams of which were angled directly upwards to form a dramatic vista in the night sky. The striking visual image this created – described as a 'cathedral of light' by Speer – was highly impactful to those who saw it becoming a powerful statement for the Reich on the national and international stage.

In September 1935, the rallies would also play a practical role in advancing Nazi racial policy, as they became the platform for announcing a series of eponymous race laws. These 'Nuremberg Laws' were hastily cobbled together for the occasion, allowing Hitler to make a signature announcement. Formally titled the 'Reich Citizenship Law' and the 'Law for the Protection of German Blood and German Honour', they were dual pieces of legislation that would prove to be a critical waypoint in the marginalisation and isolation of Germany's Jews. Their provisions laid out a crucial mechanism for the German state to define Jewish identity, and to place restrictions

Dresden was the location of a particularly devastating series of raids in February 1945. Over 25,000 people died in the firestorm that arose from the aerial assault on the city. These raids have since become a source of increasing controversy.

on sexual relationships between those they defined as 'Aryans' and 'Jews'. The laws would also form the basis for further exclusion of Jews from various professional and social spheres.

The choice of Nuremberg for the trial was therefore not only practical but symbolic, offering a figurative riposte to the Nazis and all that the city had stood for. Holding the proceedings in this former crucible of Nazism would forcefully make the case that their regime had failed. Hitler may have envisioned a thousand-year Reich, while surveying the massed ranks at his rallies there, but the Allies were keen to underline the fact that he hadn't got close – and it was now them, and not him, who would determine the future of Europe.

Despite the many factors working in its favour, however, there was no guarantee from the outset that Nuremberg would ultimately be chosen as the trial's location. The Americans were enthusiastic about the idea, and Britain and France were both supportive – partly because they agreed on its practical and symbolic virtues, and partly because they knew that holding the trial in a US zone of occupation meant access to America's superior rations and provisions. The Soviets, though, were less keen, arguing that the proceedings should be held in Berlin. Berlin was located within their occupation zone, and staging the trial there would – they believed – embolden their standing and status. After some lengthy discussions, it was ultimately agreed that the location would be Nuremberg, but, as a compromise, that the permanent seat of the IMT would be established in Berlin under the Soviets' leadership.

Albert Speer's 'Cathedral of Light' at the 1937 Nuremberg Rally.

Preparing the Stage

Though the Palace of Justice had emerged from the bombing campaign broadly intact, it was not completely unscathed. It had been hit by a bomb that hadn't detonated, and there was additional war damage that needed to be repaired before the tribunal could begin. In addition, the courtroom itself – 'Courtroom 600' – required significant modification in order to make it fit for purpose. While before the war it had been the principal courtroom in the German state of Franconia, at the time it was requisitioned it was being used as a mess hall. Not only did it no longer look much like a courtroom, it also lacked the space and technical infrastructure to meet the very specific demands of the trial. Responsibility for overseeing the repairs to the building and bringing it to readiness fell to US Army Captain Daniel Kiley.

Kiley was a 33-year-old architect from Boston. He would go on to become a significant modernist landscape architect, with many highly celebrated projects, but in 1945 he was playing his part in the war by serving as Chief of Design in the Presentation Branch in the US Office of Strategic Services. The challenge of developing the building to accommodate the tribunal presented him with a series of very particular considerations. Not only would the courtroom need to have sufficient space for the four prosecuting counsels and the defence – as well as the defendants – but it would also need to meet the requirements of the broadcast media and the interpreters. These latter two components were distinct and integral to this particular trial and, since they were both firsts, Kiley was working without precedent. Given that the tribunal would also include the screening of film clips, he would need to accommodate the infrastructure for that too.

Kiley created a model of the room to confirm his plans and to work out the positioning of the various elements involved. A soundproof box for interpreters was placed in the front corner of the courtroom and vestibules for cameramen were built into the walls. These features, however, were not the only elements of the design that were highly distinct. The decision was made to place the witness box in the centre of the space, and to put the large projection screen behind this. Locating these two elements in this way gave them a sense of being 'centre stage', creating an impression of focus and performance – both in the room and through broadcast footage. Some of the trial's most defining moments – whether that was the testimony of the defendants or the screening of atrocity film – were profoundly shaped by this framing. It's not certain if Kiley or Jackson were ultimately most instrumental in making these critical decisions, but, regardless of who was responsible, the choices had a material role to play in the way that the proceedings operated and were received.

The scale model of the courtroom in Nuremberg, which was used to show those installing the interior elements where everything should be positioned.

At work on the Court Room.

Pure Hollywood

Courtroom 600 at the Palace of Justice in the middle of modifications for the IMT.

The speed at which the rebuilding and modification of the court building was carried out struck everyone who was involved. Here in the ruins of the city, a room had emerged suitable for hosting one of the most high-profile trials of all time in a matter of months. British prosecution team member George D Roberts was one of many that was impressed, recording his thoughts in a letter saying:

> I saw it [the courtroom] in July '45. It was then small, dark utterly incapable of staging such a scene. Now it is very large: blazing lights. The USA have done a wonderful job knocking down walls: building up others. From a dignified small provincial courthouse it is now Pure Hollywood.[1]

An unexpected feature of the courthouse that also made an impression was how warm it was. After the privations of wartime service that many of those in attendance had endured, the comfort this afforded was much appreciated. Kenneth G Burton, who was part of the British delegation, noted how the central heating was kept at 'American heights of temperature', which was welcome after 'two winters in the cold, and sometimes extreme cold, and often in tents'.[2] The system was not infallible, however, and Julius Stafford-Baker, who attended Nuremberg as an artist with the RAF Public Relations Directorate, commented on the delays to the trial resulting from it breaking down.

The Hotel

A short distance from the Palace of Justice was the Grand Hotel. The facility, which had housed senior Nazis during the Nuremberg Rallies, was requisitioned by US authorities and became both a home and a social hub for the international community who convened there for the trial. Next to the Grand Hotel was a building known as the Nazi 'Guest House'. Hitler commissioned this in 1938 after becoming frustrated that the hotel couldn't accommodate all his guests for that year's rally, as it had been booked by American visitors. During

A group comprised of members from the US, British and French delegations visiting Nuremberg in July 1945. Robert Jackson is fourth from the right standing between David Maxwell Fyfe and Robert Falco (with G D Roberts behind).

preparations for the trial, the hotel and the Guest House were combined to maximise accommodation for prosecution staff.

Though the Grand Hotel was still serviceable, it had not completely escaped the ravages of the war. Alongside some superficial damage, Allied bombing had cut a large hole through a number of floors. It was not possible to repair this in time for the start of the trial, and so it remained as a challenge for guests to negotiate – particularly those whose rooms were on the other side of it and could only access their accommodation via wooden planks that straddled the cavity. Soviet interpreter George Vassiltchikov later recalled how challenging it could be returning late at night. There were no handrails or harnesses, and the drop was not inconsiderable. Vassiltchikov noted that it was difficult enough under any circumstances, but particularly after an evening spent drinking in the hotel bar, which was a regular occurrence.

The hotel was a good size, but it was not large enough to house everyone who came to the city for the IMT – even with the extension into Hitler's former Guest House. As the volume of people in Nuremberg working on the proceedings grew, accommodation therefore had to be sourced at other sites. National delegations would typically remain together in a single area in the city. Buses were provided to transport those staying at these other locations to the courtroom each day. Even for those who were based elsewhere, however, the Grand Hotel remained the social centre of the trial.

The Grand Hotel, Nuremberg, in July 1945, undergoing renovations to repair damage visible on the front face of the building.

Local Relations

The provisions on offer within the hotel were 'off the ration' and stood in radical contrast to the privations being endured elsewhere in the city. Local Germans, who were subsisting on very little, stood staring through the windows of the dining room, incredulous at the amount that those inside had to eat. Many would rifle through the bins outside the kitchen for anything that was thrown away. Some of those working on the trial found the disparity between the abundance inside the building and the struggles outside it unbearable, and ultimately chose to take their meals out of sight.

Relationships in general between the city's residents and

those who came to work on the trial changed significantly over time. The war had only recently ended, and its scars – both practical and emotional – were still fresh. When Allied staff initially arrived strict rules remained in place about fraternisation. These rules prohibited any meaningful contact between those who were there for the proceedings and the local community. Even if these were not always followed, they formalised a seemingly intractable division. Eventually, though, as restrictions were loosened things changed. In time, men working on the trial were allowed to bring German women to dance halls, which they often did, and the romantic relationships that inevitably followed fostered connections. In broader terms, while some of the city's residents remained wary of Nuremberg's visitors, others came to form close bonds with them. Despite the circumstances in which the trial was being held, Peter Calvocoressi – a British intelligence officer who served as prosecution researcher at the trial – was struck by the lack of hostility that came from the local population. He commented that, rather than being antagonistic, they generally appeared subdued and defeated.

A cafeteria card and ration card issued to K G Burton. Burton was part of No. 5 Public Relations Service and was at Nuremberg to work on media communications. The Americanised spellings and use of words such as 'candy' underpin the fact that these provisions were issued by the US.

EM MESS CARD
COURT CAFETERIA

NAME Burton, Kenneth RANK Sgt.

SIGNATURE OF BEARER

Louis P Coufos
M/SGT. IN CHARGE OF
CAFETERIA OPERATIONS NO. 1097

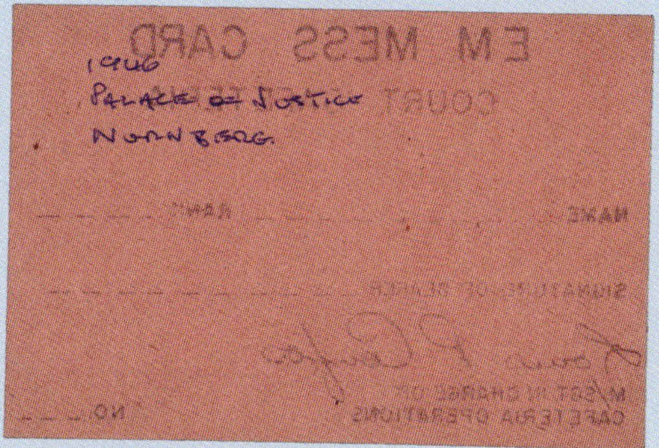

Anyone apprehended reselling, trading or bartering Post Exchange merchandise will forfeit all rights to exchange privileges and will be dealt with under the appropriate article of war.
This card is valid in all European Theater Exchanges.

C- D 36966 * I.M.T.-P.X.

ARMY EXCHANGE
RATION CARD-EUROPEAN THEATER

Date issued 23 Sept. 1946
Name BURTON K. ASN
Signature
Organization British APO
Signature Unit C.O.

AGO card or identification tag of purchaser must be presented and purchase noted on the card. No purchases are permitted unless identification is shown.

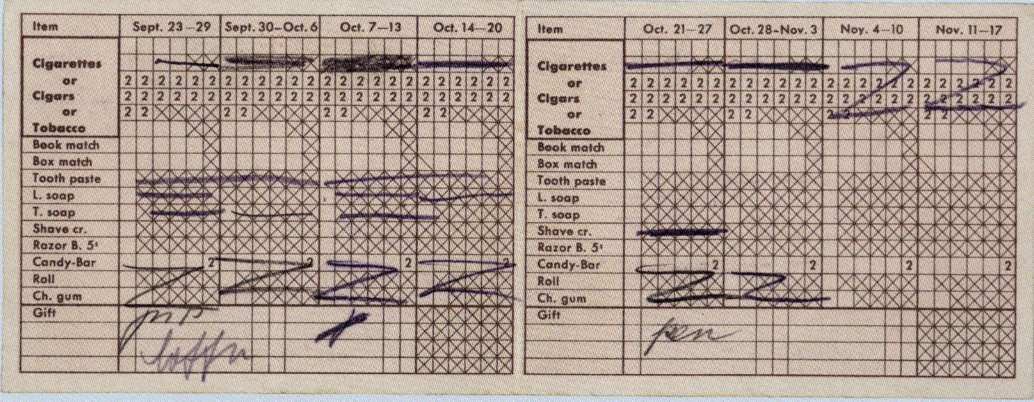

Item	Sept. 23–29	Sept. 30–Oct. 6	Oct. 7–13	Oct. 14–20
Cigarettes or Cigars or Tobacco				
Book match				
Box match				
Tooth paste				
L. soap				
T. soap				
Shave cr.				
Razor B. 5¢				
Candy-Bar	2	2	2	2
Roll				
Ch. gum				
Gift				

Item	Oct. 21–27	Oct. 28–Nov. 3	Nov. 4–10	Nov. 11–17
Cigarettes or Cigars or Tobacco				
Book match				
Box match				
Tooth paste				
L. soap				
T. soap				
Shave cr.				
Razor B. 5¢				
Candy-Bar	2	2	2	2
Roll				
Ch. gum				
Gift				

Alfred Rosenberg in his prison cell at Neumunster, just after his capture.
Founder-member of the Hitler gang. Creator of the "Aryan Creed" of the Nazis. Former Minister (and Gauleiter) for occupied Russia. Jew-baiter and organiser of the 1939 "book purge."
Eric Taylor
19 May 45.

CHAPTER THREE

The Accused

Alfred Rosenberg in his Prison Cell at Neumünster: *Just after his capture* by Eric Wilfred Taylor.

Determinations about the indictment and the shape and structure of the trial preceded any conclusions about who would actually be charged – those decisions would come next. 'The general idea', as Calvocoressi described it, 'was that you would represent in the dock all the principle agents of the German Nazi state'.[1] However, agreeing on exactly who these individuals were was not straightforward. For starters, those who would have been at the very top of the roster – Hitler, Himmler and Goebbels – were now beyond the trial's earthly reach, having escaped the process by dying by their own hands in the final throes of the war and its aftermath. Hitler shot himself in his Berlin bunker on 30 April 1945, while his propaganda minister Joseph Goebbels and his wife had overseen the murder of their six children before killing themselves the next day. Head of the SS Heinrich Himmler had nurtured hopes of escaping, but after being taken into British custody had managed to get an undetected cyanide pill into his mouth. Of those who remained, though, some defendants – Hermann Göring, for example, 'practically picked themselves',[2] as Calvocoressi described it – elsewhere things were a little less clear-cut.

Decisions about who should ultimately be chosen had to be agreed among delegates of the countries involved. To make the process of arriving at an agreed roster as equitable as possible, each of the four different prosecuting teams produced their own list of names, and from those lists the final group was chosen. There was some crossover between these lists, which made things easier, but a degree of horse trading was necessary to confirm the rest. To make matters more complicated, while the intention was that those in the stand should be a representative cross-section of Nazi leadership (military, political, economic and diplomatic), sometimes the right individual to fill these gaps no longer existed. When this happened, someone else was forced to take their place. These supposed 'deputies' were not always suitable substitutes, which caused the prosecution problems further down the line when the details about their contribution were interrogated in court.

The decision about the actual number of defendants that there should be – 24 – was not determined by any pre-existing judicial precedent but by a far more practical issue. A rough calculation suggested that all things being considered, this was the maximum that could sensibly be accommodated on the benches in the courtroom. Though apparently slightly arbitrary, there was some broader logic in the number – it was large enough to achieve the cross section of Nazism intended, but not so large that it was unmanageable. As things turned out, 24 defendants would never actually take their place in court. Martin Bormann, whose whereabouts were still unknown in November 1945, was tried in absentia. Gustav Krupp von Bohlen und Halbach, who was infirm, immobile and suffering from dementia, was eventually deemed unfit to stand trial and had the charges against him dismissed. Robert Ley died by suicide before proceedings began.

The 24 Men

Martin Bormann

Martin Bormann was central to the inner workings of the Nazi regime but maintained a more shadowy public identity. He was a long-standing member of the party having originally joined in 1927. Before becoming a Nazi he had been a member of another right wing-organisation and was convicted for a politically motivated murder in the 1920s. He worked his way through a number of positions and by the final years of the war was Hitler's deputy, controlling access to Germany's leader and using his position to advance his own interests and agendas. Bormann was last seen exiting Hitler's bunker during the fall of Berlin and his whereabouts were still unknown at the time of the trial. Later evidence would prove that he had died in the streets of the city during his attempted escape. For decades uncertainty persisted about the specific circumstances surrounding his death, but an autopsy conducted on his remains in 1972 identified glass fragments in his jaw indicating that the cause was suicide by cyanide capsule.

Karl Dönitz

Karl Dönitz was a naval officer. He was responsible for the development of Germany's U-boat fleet, having served as a submarine officer in the First World War. At the outbreak of the Second World War, he was the commander of Germany's U-boats, and in 1943 he was appointed commander-in-chief of the German Navy. Hitler designated Dönitz as his successor shortly before his suicide - though this came as a surprise to many, including Dönitz himself. During his brief time as leader, he pursued peace with the Allies, eventually sending a delegation to General Dwight D Eisenhower's headquarters, on 7 May 1945, to sign the final surrender of all German forces. Throughout the trial Dönitz attempted to style himself as a professional member of the navy, following orders in the German military tradition.

Hans Frank

Hans Frank was a lawyer, serving as Hitler's personal counsel from 1928–1933. He went on to hold a number of posts in the pre-war Nazi regime, including President of the Reichstag and Minister of Justice. After the outbreak of war, he was appointed Governor-General of the area of occupied Poland known as the *Generalgouvernement*, or General Government. In this capacity, he was responsible for the maltreatment, enslavement and murder of millions of civilians. The deportation and mass killing of Polish Jews happened across his zone of responsibility. Frank attempted to take his own life after being captured, doing permanent damage to his motor skills in one arm. Before the trial, he had a religious epiphany and expressed total remorse – though not responsibility – for the crimes that had happened under his watch. He claimed that a number of resignation attempts during the war evidenced his dismay at – and resistance to – the mass murder of millions.

Wilhelm Frick

Wilhelm Frick had been an early follower of Hitler, taking part in his ill-fated attempted coup – known as the Beer Hall Putsch – in 1923. He became a Nazi deputy in the Reichstag in 1924 and was the first Nazi minister to hold a post in a provincial government (in Thuringia in 1930). He was part of Hitler's inaugural government, serving as Reich Minister of the Interior from 1933 to 1943, before becoming Reich Protector for Bohemia and Moravia from 1943 to 1945. In this capacity, he was responsible for the development and enactment of legislation relating to the exclusion of Jews from public life, as well as the persecution of political opponents. At the IMT he tried to suggest that he was unaware that the laws he oversaw would constitute crimes.

Hans Fritzsche

Hans Fritzsche served in the propaganda ministry, assuming overall responsibility for the radio division from 1942. Relative to other defendants in the dock, he was a minor figure and was virtually unknown to the rest of the defendants, none of whom he had ever met before. His inclusion on the list of the accused at the IMT was more related to the ministry he represented than his personal role. It was also connected to the fact that he was in Soviet custody. As most prisoners had escaped west in the final days of the war and its aftermath, desperate to avoid the clutches of the Soviets, they had very few prisoners to offer

the trial; suggesting Fritzsche, therefore, had reputational value for them. Had Goebbels still been alive, Fritzsche would not have appeared.

Walther Funk

Walther Funk joined the Nazi Party in 1931, becoming an economic adviser to Hitler. During this time, he helped to develop a network of industrialists to help finance the Nazis' ambitions. He was appointed Press Chief in the Reich Government and later Under Secretary in the Ministry of Propaganda. In 1938 he took office as Minister of Economics and Plenipotentiary General for War Economy, becoming President of the Reichsbank in January 1939. He was involved with efforts to drive German Jews from the workplace and later became central to the recycling of stolen assets and property from murdered Jewish people into the German war economy. He tried to diminish his significance during the trial, claiming that he was never involved with decision-making and had no power.

Hermann Göring

Hermann Göring was a leading figure throughout the Nazi period, and at one time the second most powerful man in the Reich. Though he held various significant posts, he was probably best known as the head of the Luftwaffe (German Air Force) and Hitler's appointed successor from 1941. The ultimate failure of the Luftwaffe to outdo Allied airpower led to Hitler losing faith in Göring's capabilities. By the end of the war, his extravagant lifestyle and substance abuse had made him a shadow of his former self, and he had little remaining power. At Nuremberg Göring fashioned himself as the ringleader among the defendants. Though he claimed he considered his fate to be sealed, at times he seemed to believe he could get the better of the prosecution team and, perhaps, still save his own skin.

Rudolf Hess

Rudolf Hess was a leading member of the Nazis in the pre-war period, and Hitler's deputy. Despite his seniority, however, he was never in a position to exert significant influence over the party or its policies. This situation worsened after the outbreak of war when Hitler started to distance himself further from Hess. Desperate to recover his former status, Hess made the bizarre decision to fly to Scotland in May 1941 to seek a meeting with the Duke of Hamilton. His ultimate ambition was to agree peace with Britain, but British authorities quickly determined that he was mentally unstable and acting without authority. Hess maintained he had total amnesia by the time he arrived at Nuremberg. Though there were constant suspicions that his behaviour was disingenuous and performative, comments that he made under secret surveillance appeared to support his claim.

Alfred Jodl

Alfred Jodl was appointed Chief of the Operations Staff of the *Oberkommando der Wehrmacht* (Supreme Command of the Armed Forces) just before the German invasion of Poland. In this

role, he directed military campaigns and oversaw the methods that the German Armed Forces employed. He signed the notorious *Kommissarbefehl* (Commissar Order) in June 1941 that instructed German forces to shoot any Soviet political commissars found among captured prisoners. In 1945 Jodl ultimately signed the surrender document that formally ended the war in Europe. He argued, at the IMT, that he had only followed orders, in the way that he was obliged to as a military man and that he had not known about the crimes committed. His attempts to distance himself from orders to carry out mass murder were undone by documents carrying his name, directly linking him to the crimes.

Ernst Kaltenbrunner

Ernst Kaltenbrunner was a lawyer and longstanding member of the SS. In 1943 he succeeded the assassinated Reinhard Heydrich as head of the *Reichssicherheitshauptamt* or RSHA (SS Reich Security Main Office). In this role he had overall control of organisations such as the *Gestapo* and *Sicherheitsdienst*, or SD, as well as having senior authority over the concentration camp network. Kaltenbrunner was a central figure in the persecution and mass murder of Europe's Jews, and was feared by Nazis and his victims alike – even Himmler was said to find him intimidating. He was the only defendant placed in handcuffs before being flown to Nuremberg. During the trial, Kaltenbrunner denied any responsibility for the mass murder that occurred under his authority, despite the overwhelming volume of evidence against him.

Wilhelm Keitel

Wilhelm Keitel was appointed chief of the *Oberkommando der Wehrmacht*, or OKW, (Supreme Command of the Armed Forces) in 1938. The OKW replaced the German War Ministry and had controlled the army, navy and air force. Though Keitel was high-ranking, after Hitler assumed control of all German armed forces, his personal influence was limited in practical terms – and despite his seniority, he commanded very little respect from his peers. A number of documents relating to war crimes bore his signature, and he was culpable for collaboration between the *Wehrmacht* and the *Einsatzgruppen* (mobile execution units) during the invasion of the Soviet Union.

Gustav Krupp von Bohlen und Halbach

Gustav Krupp von Bohlen und Halbach was a diplomat who married into the Krupp family. He was appointed chairman of the family business – which specialised in the production of steel and armaments – shortly after the wedding, and eventually also became chairman of the Reich Association of Industry. The Krupp family business helped to finance the Nazis during their seizure of power and benefited significantly from orders placed by the Nazi government. As well as profiting from unlawful German rearmament and the pursuit of the war itself, they were also widescale users of slave labour. The decision to include Krupp on the list of defendants was controversial given the level of his infirmity by 1945. It would ultimately prove to be ill-conceived as he was eventually determined to be too unwell to face trial. Some believe that a mistake by prosecutors meant that the name of Gustav was entered, rather than his son Alfried – who actually ran the company during most of the war. Prosecutors attempted to submit Alfried to replace his father after Gustav had been deemed unable to stand, but the judges would not allow it.

Robert Ley

Robert Ley ran the *Deutsche Arbeitsfront*, or DAF (German Labour Front), from 1933 to 1945. This also gave him control of the *Kraft durch Freude*, or KdF (Strength Through Joy), organisation which attempted to consolidate Nazi policies and attitudes in the pre-war period through leisure activities. Ley was an unapologetically vehement and outspoken antisemite long before the Nazis assumed power. During the war, his bigotry evolved into open support for mass annihilation. The growth in Speer's authority came at the expense of Ley – as Speer assumed control of areas where Ley had been most active – but he remained a member of Hitler's inner circle. He viewed the outcome of the trial as a certainty and chose to deny the Allies the opportunity to execute him by taking his own life while in custody.

Konstantin Freiherr von Neurath

Konstantin Freiherr von Neurath served as Germany's ambassador to Britain from 1930–1932. He became Foreign Minister of Germany from 1932 to 1938 and Reich Protector of Bohemia and Moravia from 1939 to 1943. His power in this second role was greatly reduced after 1941 when Hitler appointed Heydrich as Neurath's deputy. Neurath attempted to resign but was unable to do so until two years later. He tried to claim that he was opposed to the radical measures used by the regime at the tribunal.

Franz von Papen

Franz von Papen was a significant political figure in post-First World War Germany. He was eventually appointed chancellor for a brief period in 1932 and was instrumental in allowing Hitler to assume the role at the start of the following year. Von Papen became Vice-Chancellor in the early period of the Nazi regime, before resigning in July 1934. He then served as ambassador to Austria – where he assisted in preparations for the *Anschluss* (the annexation of Austria by Germany) – before becoming ambassador to Turkey. Von Papen was adamant that he didn't carry any responsibility for the crimes of the Nazis, despite the part he had played in Hitler coming to power.

Erich Raeder

Erich Raeder had joined the *Kriegsmarine* (German Navy) in 1896. In 1935 he was appointed its Commander in Chief, and in 1939 he was made Grand Admiral – a role that Hitler created. He remained in this position until his resignation and retirement in May 1943, when he was forced to step down due to his differing views on strategy with Hitler. Raeder tried to dissociate himself from the crimes of the Nazi regime by claiming they had happened outside his sphere of responsibilities. The decision to include him on the list of defendants was met with some resistance among Allied naval representatives.

Joachim von Ribbentrop

Joachim von Ribbentrop was an adviser to Hitler on foreign affairs during the 1930s and was German ambassador to Britain from 1936 to 1938. He was appointed Foreign Minister of Germany from 1938 to 1945. In this capacity, he played the key role in negotiating the German-Soviet non-aggression pact bearing his name, which enabled the German invasion of Poland in September 1939. He was also actively involved in diplomatic efforts to persuade Germany's allies to deport Jews in their territories to Nazi killing centres and to allow the deportation of their Jewish citizens living in Germany. At Nuremberg he claimed that he had no responsibility for any of the decisions that Hitler made and had only ever wanted peace.

Alfred Rosenberg

Alfred Rosenberg was a virulently antisemitic ideologue who was very influential on Hitler in the early years of the Nazis. He developed a reputation as the Nazis' philosopher, encapsulating his ideas in the 1934 book *The Myth of the*

Twentieth Century. He became head of the party's foreign affairs department in 1933, remaining in this post until 1945. In 1941 he was appointed Reich Minister for the Occupied Eastern Territories. In this role he had responsibility for German policy in occupied areas of the Soviet Union. This included the annihilation of Soviet Jews and the deportation of millions of non-Jewish Soviet civilians for forced labour in Germany. At the IMT, he claimed that the radicalisation of the regime had been the fault of others.

Fritz Sauckel

Fritz Sauckel was a longstanding member of the Nazi Party and an ardent admirer of Hitler. In 1927 he became *Gauleiter* (regional leader) in Thuringia and a leading secretary of state in Germany's first National Socialist government in 1932. When he was appointed Plenipotentiary General for Labour Deployment in 1942, he became responsible for supplying forced labourers to meet Germany's increasing war production needs. Under his authority, the Germans deported millions of forced labourers from occupied territories to the Reich. At the trial, he attempted to suggest that there was no systemic maltreatment or exploitation of these labourers.

Hjalmar Schacht

Hjalmar Schacht was Minister of Economics and General Plenipotentiary for the War Economy until 1937 and Reichsbank (national bank) president until 1939. He was largely responsible for Germany's remarkable economic revival in the early years of the Nazi regime, but never joined the party. He remained Minister without Portfolio after being succeeded by Göring as Reichsbank president, but was sent to a concentration camp in 1944 due to his association with resistance members involved in the attempted assassination of Hitler in the so-called July plot. Schact was incandescent about the accusations that were levelled at him at the trial, particularly given the position he was in by the end of the war.

Baldur von Schirach

Baldur von Schirach was leader of the Hitler Youth from 1931. By 1936 the organisation had over six million members, giving Schirach an influential role in the indoctrination of Germany's young people. In 1940 he was also appointed Reich Governor and *Gauleiter* in Vienna. During his time in office, 65,000 Jews were deported from Vienna to ghettos and camps in occupied Poland. Although, at the IMT, he confessed his role in the propagation of Nazi ideology, he denied being aware of the mass murder of Jews.

Arthur Seyss-Inquart

Arthur Seyss-Inquart was a successful Austrian lawyer before formally entering politics in 1937. After the Nazis assumed control of Austria, he held various roles, but it was as *Reichskommissar* (Reich Commissioner) for the German-occupied Netherlands that he wielded most authority. During his tenure, up to 140,000 Dutch Jews were deported, the majority of whom were murdered. He also oversaw the savage anti-resistance policies and the shooting of hostages. At the tribunal, Seyss-Inquart claimed he continually attempted to mitigate the impact of Nazi policy on the people under his charge.

Albert Speer

Albert Speer was Hitler's personal architect. In 1942 he was appointed Minister of Armaments and in 1943 Minister for Armaments and War Production. This gave him significant status within the regime and ultimate responsibility for the German war economy. His operations made extensive use of forced and slave labourers, many of whom died. Speer was keen to acknowledge what he saw as liability by association, but strove to distance himself from the war crimes themselves. He claimed he had been unaware of systemic maltreatment, violence and mass murder, and was the only defendant to show meaningful contrition – though how authentic this was remains controversial.

Julius Streicher

Julius Streicher was the creator and publisher of the violently antisemitic newspaper *Der Stürmer*, alongside a range of other anti-Jewish pamphlets and books. Though he had no political power – and had been broadly sidelined by 1940 – he was a central figure in the Nazis' persecution of Jewish people. The challenge for Allied prosecutors was to establish a clear relationship between his activities and the actions of others. His anti-Jewish hostility was not what he was in the dock for and, to secure a conviction, it was necessary to prove liability for the crimes in question. Streicher was unrepentant during the trial, peppering his responses with antisemitic diatribes directed towards the prosecution and the court.

Capture

By the time the list of defendants was confirmed, all except Martin Bormann were in the hands of the Allies. As most senior Nazis had headed west as the Reich collapsed, the majority were prisoners of the British and Americans, having been arrested in the weeks after the German surrender. Some of those in custody were picked up as part of targeted operations, while others found themselves captured through more general roundups.

Ernst Kaltenbrunner was tracked down in Tyrol, Austria, where he had fled to, by men from the 80th Counter Intelligence Corps (CIC) as part of an operation to take him in. He had been identified through his mistress, Gisela von Westarp, who had been seen in the area. To make the arrest, the CIC unit had to navigate through mounds of snow, for five hours, to the Alpine cabin where he was hiding out. They were guided on this challenging journey by four former members of the *Wehrmacht*. When they eventually arrived, the troops were concerned about how exposed their position was and how little cover it afforded them. At one stage they feared the raid would end in a violent confrontation, but Kaltenbrunner eventually surrendered without a shot being fired.

Arthur Seyss-Inquart, meanwhile, was arrested on the Elbe Bridge in Hamburg, Germany, by soldiers of the Royal Welch Fusiliers. One of those involved was Norman Miller, a German Jew (born Norbert Müller) originally from Nuremberg, who had arrived in the UK on a *Kindertransport* at the age of 15, just two days before the outbreak of war. Norman's mother and father, Sebald and Laura, and younger sister, Suse, had been unable to leave Germany and were all later murdered by the Nazis. Norman joined the British Army in 1944 and was sent to Belgium in 1945, starting as an infantryman before he was transferred to headquarters for intelligence work once it became known he was fluent in German. He was in Hamburg at the time of the German surrender, where he was tasked with controlling traffic on the bridges. After examining the papers of those in a limousine that was trying to pass, he realised that one of the passengers was the former Reich Commissar of the Netherlands.

Three of the men who would become defendants were arrested in a single swoop by British servicemen during an operation to dismantle the so-called Flensburg government, which had briefly assumed control of Germany after the death of Hitler. On 23 May 1945, soldiers from the Hertfordshire and Cheshire regiments raided the interim administration's headquarters as part of Operation 'Blackout'. They achieved complete surprise and were able to secure a significant number of prisoners. Among them were Jodl, Speer and Dönitz.

Allied teams conducting the arrests quickly learned to intercede swiftly in any suicide attempts made by the prisoners. As these attempts tended to rely on using cyanide vials, as soon as suspects were in range, arresting teams would secure their wrists to prevent them from placing anything in their mouths. They would then be subject to a full cavity search to ensure that nothing was hidden elsewhere. The Allies had grasped the necessity of being thorough with this process the hard way. Himmler, most notably, while secure in British custody, had been able to kill himself using a vial concealed in his mouth,

Norman Miller stands with his rifle and helmet while serving with the Royal Welch Fusiliers.

Albert Speer, Karl Dönitz and Alfred Jodl after their arrest by British forces as part of Operation 'Blackout'.

which wasn't discovered until he opted to bite on it.

Dr Robert Thompson was Senior Medical Officer in the British Army in northern Germany when he became involved with the arrest of Joachim von Ribbentrop. In a letter written to his wife a few days later, Thompson described how he had been called to ensure that the prisoner had not hidden any unseen amulets. After examining his mouth, Thompson ordered Ribbentrop to undress. He described how Ribbentrop grabbed at something 'strapped to an "intimate" portion of his anatomy', telling his captor, 'if you are looking for poison I will save you the trouble. There it is.'[3] Mindful that there could be further vials, Thompson conducted a full internal examination, admitting that he 'wasn't very gentle'[4] while doing so. He describes how he had been struck by the way Ribbentrop's arrogance faded during the process.

H.Q. 8 Base Sub Area
B.L.A.
Sat 16 Jun

My Darling Sally,

I had no letters yesterday – only the Sphere which, of course, was much appreciated.

As you will have heard, Ribbentrop was captured in Hamburg on Thursday morning. A message was sent to our H.Q. asking for a senior medical officer to go and examine an important person. I was sent along. When I got there I was told who it was. In a way I had guessed who it might be. What a thrill!

I told them what I intended to do – our fear was, of course, that as soon as he knew he was going to be examined, he would try to swallow poison. In we went and there he was – much fatter than he used to be, and plus a moustache. First I stuck my fingers in his mouth and had a good look around – nothing there. Then I ordered him to take off his jacket, waistcoat, and shirt. As he took his things off I sent them out of the room. (Two security officers were present with me when all this was going on.) He didn't like parting with his shirt! I examined him very carefully. He kept on saying "What are you looking for? Are you looking for poison?" I didn't answer him, but just went on. Then I told him to take his trousers off. I got the two security officers to hold his hands, but he suddenly pulled one hand away and pushed it down between his legs! I grabbed hold of his wrist and he said "if you are looking for poison, I will save you the trouble – there it is." He opened his hand and there was a little round sealed tin with adhesive plaster on it. It had been strapped to an intimate portion of his anatomy and must have been very painful, judging from the appearance of the skin. The atmosphere was absolutely terrific, and I have never been so excited in all my life! I then got his socks and shoes off, and made him get down on his hands and knees stark naked, and examined him per rectum. There was no poison there! He didn't like that a bit. As I was doing this examination I thought to myself that this was the man who said we were a decadent degenerate people, and that this was the man who gave the King the Nazi salute, and I wasn't very gentle in my examination. He groaned and moaned, and made a fuss, but that didn't stop me!

We then gave him a pair of long pants and a vest – his own, which I had previously inspected. He also got a pair of thick pyjamas to put on, but they offended his dignity too much, and he wouldn't wear them. I said to him "if you feel cold, you'll be glad to put them on." I left him sitting there in a chair, with his head sunk in his hands, a tragic figure [illegible] ever there was one.

I have one interesting souvenir, an[d] saw the letters which he wrote to Monty [and] Winston Churchill. The latter was addressed as Vincent Churchill.

Ribbentrop doesn't seem to think that he will be treated as a war criminal. Despite his tragic position, he is still arrogant. It was only when we took all his clothes off, and submitted him to a close, personal examination, that he lost his arrogant bearing.

The wireless today says that doctors examined him and found poison. That isn't so. I was the only person there apart from the security officers. He left here yesterday.

It was my big moment, and I shall never forget it. Both the security officers and I were literally trembling with excitement when we found the poison.

One of the security officers got an interesting souvenir! I wouldn't let Ribbentrop put his own shoes on again, in case there should be a dummy heel or anything of that [sor]t, so the security officer swopped shoes [wit]h him, and, so far as I know, has still [got] Ribbentrop's.

Keep this letter, Sally, as a memento of my big day. Tell Do and Mary – they will be thrilled.

I still haven't got over the excitement.

Give my love to all in Primavera. I do hope Auntie and Mary are getting out and feeling better for the change.

And please give my wee darling a kiss from their silly old daddy.

All my love, sweetheart,
Yours ever,
Bobbie.

In Custody

A letter written by Dr Robert Thompson to his wife, Sally, in June 1945 while he was serving as a Medical Officer with the British Liberation Army in northern Germany. In the letter he describes his examination of the former Nazi Foreign Minister Joachim von Ribbentrop.

The defendants were transferred to Nuremberg in October 1945. After their arrival, responsibility for the day-to-day management of their custody sat with the Americans – though security for the exterior of the Grand Palace remained the responsibility of the four nations involved. US Army Colonel Burton C Andrus was commandant of the prison, and was tasked with ensuring that all of those in the cells were fit to stand trial. Andrus took his role seriously, and in turn earned the respect of both the defendants and his own peers. Though he knew it was likely that at least a few of those he was in charge of would be executed, he wanted to ensure that they were in the best health possible when this happened. A report sent from the trial commented 'it seemed…his one object in life was to keep the accused in a healthy condition to meet their ultimate fate'.[5]

A perennial concern for Andrus was the ongoing threat of suicide. To thwart any potential attempts, prisoners had no access to anything that might be used as a ligature and were under constant surveillance. Even spectacles were confiscated from cells at night to prevent their lenses being removed and broken into pieces that could be used to slit wrists.

Despite this rigorous approach, however, the system was not failproof and Ley managed to hang himself shortly before proceedings commenced. This incident caused Andrus considerable dismay. In a report compiled shortly afterwards, he stated: 'The Corporal discovered prisoner Ley seated on the toilet, his mouth stuffed with rags apparently torn from his own underwear. Around his neck was the hemmed edge of a towel fastened to the top of the toilet flushpipe.'[6] Ley had concealed the attempt by positioning himself on the toilet so that his knees were still visible to guards. This only alerted suspicion when it was noted he hadn't moved for an unusually long period.

After Ley's suicide, Andrus was determined that there would be no others. He adjusted procedures so that a single guard was stationed on every cell door. Prisoners were forced to lie on their backs at night with their hands above the covers and had to endure regular torchlight on their faces as they slept.

In addition to suicide, the prison's authorities were

also concerned about the prospect of 'lone wolf'[7] assassins breaching the security cordon and gaining access to the defendants. There were a vast number of people who had significant motivations for wanting to get their hands on those in the cells, and Andrus's team had to ensure that didn't happen.

Despite the strict security put in place to protect those standing trial, some defendants were convinced that it wasn't assassins from outside that they needed to worry about but a threat from within. Hess was certain that he was being slowly poisoned, attributing his stomach pains and memory loss to substances being added to his meals, and was not the only one who worried that their gaolers were trying to kill them rather than care for them.

As part of the stringent surveillance the prisoners were kept under, all mail to and from the defendants was read by Allied authorities. Responsibility for this job fell to a young soldier called Howard Triest, who was also tasked with censoring the correspondence and providing general translation as required in the prison. Howard – who had been born Hans – was another of the many Jewish refugees recruited to work in the trial. He had fled from the Nazis' antisemitic persecution in Germany with his parents and sister. The family were able to get as far as Luxembourg before their funds ran out. The parents, Berthold and Lena, eventually managed to get Hans and their daughter, Margot, to safety but despite desperate efforts were unable to escape themselves. In August 1942, they were sent to Drancy transit camp in France, from where they were deported to Auschwitz and murdered. Hans made his way to America where he changed his name and became a US citizen in 1943. Through his role at the IMT, he was handling letters written by those who been culpable for what had happened to his parents, as well as sitting in on interviews with them, translating what they were saying. In later life, he would say that he took some satisfaction from this reversal of status.

Though it was the intention of the prison authorities to keep the defendants healthy, the conditions in which they were kept came as a shock after the privileges they had enjoyed as senior members of the Nazi state. They were given the same meagre allowance of calories as the rest of the German

These instructions, issued by Colonel Andrus prior to the defendants' arrival, set out procedures for the care and confinement of prisoners.

K66711

HEADQUARTERS
INTERNAL SECURITY DETACHMENT
OFFICE, U. S. CHIEF OF COUNSEL
APO 403, U.S. ARMY

2 September 1945.

STEPS TAKEN TO PREPARE FOR CONFINEMENT OF THE

WAR CRIMINALS

1. Iron hooks and projections removed from all cells.

2. Replacement of all glass window panes with cello-glass.

3. Removal of all weapons or instruments which might be used for suicide or self harm completed for each prisoner upon his arrival.

4. German doctor on duty in cell block 24 hours per day. (40 years professional practice) Treatment prescribed by American army doctor who visits internees daily.

5. Dentist provided in the cell block. All dental work kept up to date. Equipment and training permits every care except construction of dentures.

6. Equipment adequate for all First Aid nearby. An Army dispensary with complete medicines available on call in three minutes.

7. All meals prepared in the cell block under US Army standards of sanitation by German prisoners of war interned for that purpose. All exper cooks brought from Mondorf. Meals served to internees in their cells, in US Army meat cans and canteen cups without handles, and only a spoon with no (repeat no) knife or fork. Food passed in under supervision of sentinel and dishes passed out under supervision of sentinel to prevent communicatio and passage of contrabands, including notes.

8. Fresh canteen cup full of treated drinking water kept in each cell throughout the day and replenished periodically under supervision of a guard.

9. Each cell contains a sanitary flush toilet, straw mattress and plenty of blankets. Prisoners are provided woolen stockings. Felt boots are provided in case trials extend into severely cold weather.

10. Each cell contains a flimsey table not capable of being stood upon. All internees are provided with all the writing paper and pencils they desire and are encouraged to write. They write letters to their relatives which in all cases are forwarded to proper authority requesting posting. They write letters to the Commandant and to the Chief of Counsel. Much of this has interrogation value and is promptly sent to the chief of interrogation.

-1-

R 64711

HEADQUARTERS
6850th INTERNAL SECURITY DETACHMENT
INTERNATIONAL MILITARY TRIBUNAL

10 November 1945

SUBJECT: Prisoner Routine, Nurnberg Jail.

TO : Personnel Concerned.

1. The prisoners are awakened each morning shortly before breakfast by the noise of the changing Guard.

2. Before breakfast is served, fresh water for washing purposes is brought and the old water disposed of by trusted P.W.Labor.

3. Breakfast is served at 0700 hours by a P.W. laborer from the kitchen who passes the food through the port in the door in a U.S.Army Meat Can with one piece of silverware, a<u>SPOON</u>, and the drink for that meal is served in an Army Canteen Cup without a handle. When meat or other food which requires a knife is served, it is so prepared in the kitchen that it can be eaten with a spoon. After the Prisoner has finished with his meal, the attendant returns and gets the empty Mess Kit, making sure that every piece is returned.

4. Soon after breakfast, another P.W. laborer brings a broom and mop so that the Prisoner can clean his cell. (Each prisoner is responsible for keeping his own cell clean.)

5. Next a P.W.laborer brings fresh (chlorinated) drinking water, or on very cold days, mid-morning coffee is served.

6. After this comes the barber who shaves each Prisoner with a safety razor. (The barber is responsible for every piece of his equipment including all old blades). At no time are conversations allowed between the German P.W.s and the Prisoners. And, at all times every occurrance is under the supervision of an American Soldier Guard.

7. During the morning or afternoon the German Doctor comes for his checkup. Should a Prisoner need medical care, he is taken to the dispensary where he receives treatment. Or should he need dental treatment, he is escorted to the Dental Clinic in the Prison where a German Dentist administers to his ailment. All of this is under the supervision of a Guard. In addition to the medical and dental care given by the German Doctors, an American Army Doctor is on duty at all times in the Prison, and this doctor views each Prisoner once each day.

8. At noon the food is brought and served in the same manner as at all other meals.

-1-

population were entitled to and were kept alone in solitary cells once they had been served their indictments. They were also expected to keep their cells presentable, and up to the standards determined by Andrus.

None of the men in Nuremberg had a more radical fall from grace than Göring. The former head of the Luftwaffe had become almost completely consumed by his lavish lifestyle in the latter years of the war. When he surrendered to Allied authorities on 7 May, he was accompanied by numerous monogrammed suitcases, stuffed with a range of products, objects and substances. Among his belongings, his captors discovered 20,000 pills, which Göring claimed had been prescribed for a heart condition. On proper inspection, it transpired they were painkillers, with similar properties to codeine. Göring had developed a dependency on the drugs and, though his intake was severely curtailed during his time in custody, it was feared if it was stopped entirely his body would buckle under the weight of withdrawal. Aside from any specific considerations arising from treating his drug use, he was placed under the same regime as the other defendants. Ironically, the stringent nature of the way that his incarceration was managed led to a noticeable improvement in both his overall health and mental acuity.

Colonel Andrus issued these instructions on 10 November 1945, just over a week before the start of the trial. Some of the stipulations evidence his concern about further suicide attempts after the death of Ley.

Defendants

The defendants at the IMT sat in the dock facing the same set of charges in relation to the same crimes, but each was ultimately tried as an individual. Though they were bound by their connection to the Nazi state, they remained a disparate group. Relationships between them were shaped by a range of internal dynamics. Göring was the self-styled leader, who was determined at the outset to maintain a common front and to use his seniority, as well as the force of his personality, to corral those around him into complying with his will. He became so successful at doing this that the authorities in the prison eventually became concerned about the control he exerted over the other inmates and the threat that this represented to the integrity of the trial. After a while, they separated him from them during meal and leisure times to temper his domineering influence.

While some defendants formed close alliances, others, such as Kaltenbrunner, Streicher and Hess, had fewer such connections. Kaltenbrunner's bearing and reputation for ruthlessness caused the others to be wary of him and keep their distance. Streicher repulsed the guards and his peers alike through his insistence on conducting his daily exercises completely naked. The obsessiveness of his antisemitism – and his determination to constantly assert it – also seemed to wear on those around him; not because they found his ideology offensive, but because it was tedious and did them no favours with their defence. Hess, meanwhile, had become both unreliable and an embarrassment with his amnesia, nonsensical outbursts and bouts of hysterical laughter.

One thing that did unify most of the defendants was their refusal to acknowledge the legitimacy of the trial – whether or not it received their support, or met their approval, they ultimately had no choice but to co-operate. Roberts KC, who was part of the British prosecution team, was fascinated by the way in which they eventually fell in line. Recording his thoughts on the first few days of proceedings, he wrote, 'It is astonishing how the Defendants have accepted the authority of this Artificial Politically-Constituted Court...these are the SUPER MEN who a few short months ago were ruling the World and acknowledging no authority except Adolf!!'[8]

From the Allies' perspective, if the trial was to fulfil its function of speaking to posterity, it was critical that it should stand up to scrutiny as fair and legitimate. The judges took their role in this seriously and held the prosecutors to rigorous standards. While, some defendants remained certain that the process was a formality that had to be endured before they were ultimately executed, there were others who hoped that there was still a chance of escaping such an eventuality. For military men, such as Göring and Jodl, the principal concern was less the sentence than the manner of their execution. They were determined that when the verdict was eventually decided, they should meet their end by firing squad, considering this to be befitting of their status. The idea of hanging – which had been mooted as the Allies' chosen method – was complete anathema to them, and quite literally a fate worse than death.

Alfred Jodl in Allied custody after his capture by men of 'A' Company, 1st Battalion, The Cheshire Regiment.

Ernst Kaltenbrunner tried to take his own life by ingesting poison on the night of his transfer to Nuremberg. His attempt failed.

CHAPTER FOUR

The Prosecution

Lord Justice Geoffrey Lawrence at the Nuremberg trial.

The prosecution team assembled for the IMT was formed of representatives from the four Allied powers. Many of these individuals had been involved in the development of the tribunal from the outset, shaping its charges, terms and processes. When the time came to make formal appointments to the court there was some uncertainty as to who among them would ultimately be appointed judges and who would be appointed prosecutors, as some could feasibly have been either. Robert Jackson, for example, had initially anticipated being anointed as his country's judge given his centrality to the creation and establishment of the IMT. In the event, President Truman opted to confer that role on Francis Biddle – who had recently stepped down as Attorney General – and named Jackson as the US chief prosecutor instead.

The nature of these appointments meant that some of the judges had been personally involved in the development of the same legal frameworks and processes that they would then be asked to adjudicate on. In the normal order of things, this might have caused some concern – at the very least it was a potential conflict of interest – but at the time nobody raised any serious objections. It appears there was total confidence that being involved in the authorship of the charges would not impact the judges' ability to remain objective and impartial.

In practical terms, each defendant needed to have a separate case prepared against them. This represented a considerable amount of administrative work, so to avoid duplicating effort the decision was made to divide the names across the prosecutors. Each prosecution team would take responsibility for assembling the case against an agreed sub-list of defendants. They would then lead the case against these individuals in court, though every country would have the opportunity for cross-examination.

As the trial date drew nearer, a series of technical questions presented themselves, generally revolving around the issue of balancing the interests of the four prosecution teams. Each was determined to ensure that they maintained their status alongside their peers. There was never any real doubt, however, about who would deliver the opening speech. Jackson – who had been so integral to proceedings from the outset – would have the honour. The three other nations would follow, but it would be Jackson who issued the first salvo.

The British prosecution team was initially led by David Maxwell Fyfe, who had recently been appointed Attorney-General in Churchill's caretaker administration. By the time of the trial itself, though, a change in government had altered Britain's political landscape. Churchill's Conservative Party had lost the election, and a Labour administration had come into power. As incoming Attorney-General, Sir Hartley Shawcross formally assumed the role of Chief Prosecutor but retained Maxwell Fyfe as his deputy – in part to demonstrate that the proceedings were bipartisan from Britain's point of view. As things turned out, pressing domestic matters meant that Shawcross was unable to dedicate his singular attention to the IMT. He fulfilled his core responsibilities – including delivering the UK's opening speech – but left the day to day running to Maxwell Fyfe. This meant that, though technically second in command, on a practical basis Maxwell Fyfe remained the *de facto* British lead. In different hands this division of responsibilities could have been difficult, but with the personalities involved it caused no issues. The two men knew each other well, having worked closely together throughout their professional lives, and were able to co-operate effectively in pursuit of their shared objective.

France's prosecution team was initially led by François de Menthon, who had served as a captain in the French Army after the outbreak of war. He was wounded and captured during his country's defeat, before escaping and becoming active

The senior British prosecution team. Rear row: Major J H Barrington; Major Elwyn Jones MP; E G Robey; Lieutenant Colonel M Griffith-Jones MC; Colonel H J Phillimore. Front row: The Right Honourable Sir David Maxwell Fyfe KC MP; HM Attorney-General Sir Hartley Shawcross KC, MP and G D Roberts KC.

within the Resistance. He eventually made his way to London to join Free French leader General Charles de Gaulle and was appointed Minister of Justice by the provisional government formed by de Gaulle in September 1944. He was given his role at Nuremberg the following year, but resigned in January 1946 to pursue a career in politics. His replacement, Auguste Champetier de Ribes, had also been active in the Resistance and manged to escape from German custody. Unfortunately, de Ribes was suffering from cancer which affected his ability to play an active role in the proceedings.

The Soviet prosecution was led by Roman Rudenko, who was Procurator-General of the Ukrainian Soviet Socialist Republic. Rudenko had Stalin's trust and was an ardent communist. The Soviets' perception of the law – and how the process at Nuremberg in particular – should work differed significantly from the other nations, but they dutifully followed the conventions of the process as agreed. The Soviet lead prosecutors were members of the military, unlike their peers from the other nations who were all professional civilian lawyers in peacetime, and wore army uniforms rather than judicial robes. While Stalin wasn't personally present, those doing his bidding were clearly operating in service of his will and considered that the verdicts were a given, having determined all the defendants were guilty before a word of the trial had been heard. Despite these differences of perspective, a strong bond formed between the Soviet prosecutors and their other Allied colleagues.

Lead British prosecutor and UK Attorney-General Hartley Shawcross (left) with G D Roberts.

George 'Khaki' Roberts famously said, 'I am told that this film will go all round the world in news reels etc, so if I don't get a job in Hollywood after this, all I can say is, I bloody well ought to.'

Team Members

Each Chief Prosecutor was at the head of a team that numbered hundreds – though the American delegation was easily the largest. Alongside the lawyers that helped to form the cases, some of whom would also have their turn in court, there were reams of staff to manage the considerable administrative work involved, ranging from the assembly and cataloguing of evidence to the translation and dissemination of documents.

The lawyers had to spend a great deal of time in each other's company, and so good working relationships were essential. Among those who made up the British team, none was more

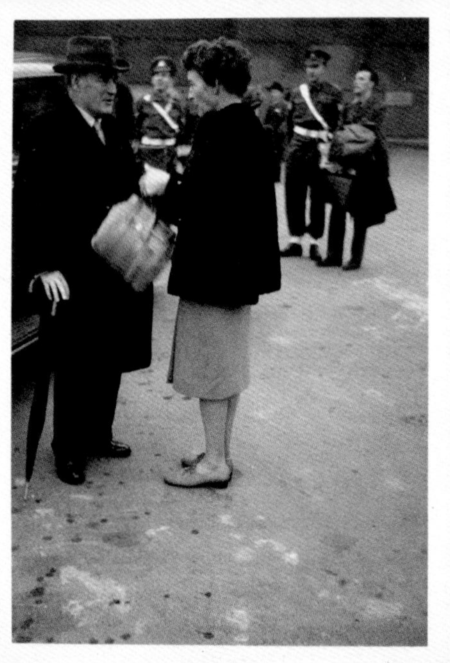

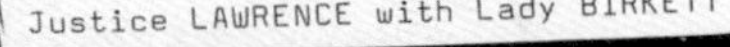

Justice LAWRENCE with Lady BIRKETT

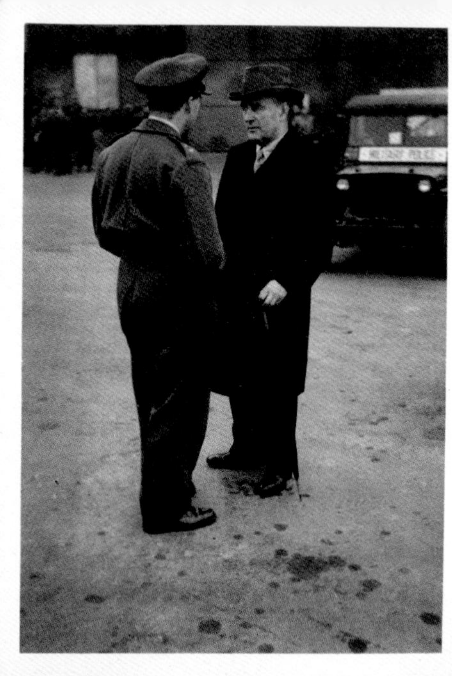

AIREY NEAVE /G.LAWRENCE

popular than Leading Counsel G D Roberts KC – better known to his contemporaries as 'Khaki Roberts'. Roberts had made three appearances for the England rugby team before being admitted to the Bar in 1912. At Nuremberg he was valued for his wit and unfailing sense of humour. He would eventually return home before the trial's end (in an attempt to reduce costs), but his presence was highly valued while he was there. In some typically irreverent thoughts he jotted down, after the first four days of proceedings, he commented, 'The German barristers are respectful, dignified and correct; but that of course is the training of our profession in all countries and you must have often noticed those qualities in me.'[1]

Among the support staff, Airey Neave, a member of the British team had a particularly significant role to play. Neave was something of a war hero, having been the first British officer to successfully escape from Colditz POW camp.

Recruited by MI9, a branch of Second World War military intelligence tasked with assisting evaders and escapers from enemy captivity, he had gone on to work on many undercover operations. It was for the skills picked up earlier in life, however, that he found himself involved with the IMT. Before the war, he had read law at Oxford and had spent time as a teenager in Germany, learning the language. His legal training and linguistic fluency made him a valuable member of the British War Crimes Executive. As part of his responsibilities in Nuremberg, he was tasked with serving the indictments to the defendants on 18 October 1945. Entering their cells in sequence, he read the document to each individual and confirmed that they understood it. It was a momentous stage in the trial.

Among the team that the Americans assembled were two mental health professionals who would go on to be closely associated with the trial for the remainder of their careers. Douglas Kelley was a psychiatrist who was brought on board to oversee the wellbeing of the prisoners and to assess their suitability for prosecution. Gustave Gilbert was a psychologist and fluent German speaker whose initial role was to maintain the morale of the prisoners and to work as a translator, but who eventually became – with his superiors' permission – the prison psychologist. During the course of their time in Nuremberg, both men became fascinated with the broader questions that the defendants posed – not just about the crimes in question but about the nature of evil itself.

As a psychiatrist, Kelley was an adherent of the Rorschach test, which had been developed by the Swiss psychiatrist Hermann Rorschach after the First World War. The test is based on the subjects' descriptions of a range of ten different ink blots on separate pieces of paper. Kelley was considered an expert in its use and believed that it could reveal critical psychological details about his subjects.

The psychiatrist developed a particular fascination with Göring, with whom he developed a close bond. The initial focus of their relationship had been Kelley's efforts to wean Göring off his dependency on paracodeine. In his notes, the doctor described how he had done this by leveraging Göring's ego, suggesting that it was only a man with his sort of strength that

Geoffrey Lawrence with Lady Birkett.

Airey Neave in conversation with Geoffrey Lawrence.

would be capable of kicking the habit. As they spent more time together, the psychiatrist involved himself with matters that were well beyond his brief – notably, intervening on Göring's behalf to reunite the Reich Marshal's wife Emmy and daughter Edda, who had become separated. He also personally delivered letters between Emmy and her husband. It appears that this connection was felt mutually, and at one stage Göring even mooted the idea that Kelley should adopt Edda and raise her in the US if anything was to happen to Emmy (though this proposal was never tested and Kelley's response is unknown).

However, despite their closeness – and the risk that the nature of the association between the two men risked blurring the line between the personal and professional – Kelley's allegiance ultimately remained with his own side. This was demonstrated most clearly in his willingness to use his role as a confidante to pass information from his patient to the prosecution in a manner that would ordinarily have been prohibited by patient and doctor confidentiality. Through his conversations, he was able to disclose such details as what defence strategy Göring was planning to use and some of his anticipated tactics.

Gustave Gilbert was brought to Nuremberg by Andrus to assist with psychological evaluation. As the son of Austrian Jewish immigrants to America, he spoke German, which meant that he was able to speak to the defendants directly in their own language. Though he made use of some of the same methods employed by Kelley – the Rorschach test, for example – his general approach was to assess his subjects through conversation. He would engage in ostensibly informal discussion in daily visits to their cells or during mealtimes, and then write up his conclusions about the interactions later on.

Though they shared similar professional interests, Kelley and Gilbert did not enjoy a good relationship, professionally or personally. Each believed that the defendants were legally sane, but analysed the root causes of their behaviour and actions differently. Kelley saw no evidence that the men were suffering from any form of mental illness, and they had therefore retained the capacity to understand what they were doing was wrong, indicating that such conduct was possible from anyone. Gilbert, on the other hand, believed that they

Psychiatrist Gustave M Gilbert in conversation with Hermann Göring and a defence counsel at Nuremberg.

Hermann Göring's counsel, Dr Otto Stahmer, is introduced to a roomful of news correspondents before the start of the trial at Nuremberg. Stahmer believed in his client's innocence and wanted to find a route to acquittal.

demonstrated traits consistent with a form of psychopathy and that this – along with a cultural deference to authority and the influence of Nazi ideology – significantly informed their actions. Initial plans for Kelley and Gilbert to write a book together reflecting their conclusions, based on their interactions with the Nuremberg defendants, were abandoned and both men released individual publications detailing their thoughts. Kelley's life ended in tragedy when he died by suicide in 1958 at the age of 45, having been unable fully to step out of the trial's shadow. After an argument with his wife he bit down on a cyanide capsule, the same method of death that his patient Göring had chosen some 12 years previously.

The day-to-day oversight of the British team fell to Lieutenant Colonel Hugh Dalton Turrall, who was Officer Commanding, British War Crimes Executive (European Section). Writing to Turrall after a visit in April 1946, General Sir Ronald Adam commented, 'You have had a very interesting and unusual task to perform, which I know has presented many problems and difficulties. You are also an isolated British detachment in a foreign country working alongside our Allies.'[2] This was certainly true. Turrall was another individual co-ordinating arrangements in an unprecedented and challenging set of circumstances. His responsibilities as Quartermaster Sergeant ran from sourcing housing and bedding to tracking down cutlery and glasses – and virtually everything in between. Though highly competent, he developed a reputation for being a stickler for the rules, which sometimes caused friction between him and those in the lower ranks. On one occasion Maxwell Fyfe became so concerned that Turrall wasn't providing sufficient entertainment for members of the team that he took it upon himself to arrange a party on behalf of the prosecutors. Despite these occasional issues, however, it is clear that his efforts were broadly well received – as Adam observed, 'All those of our Allies whom I met spoke very highly of the work that you and your unit have done'.[3]

A particularly important appointment that affected the trial in its entirety was the selection of British judge Geoffrey Lawrence as the court's president. The post, which had both practical and symbolic significance, gave him a tie-breaking vote in the convictions and a position of unimpeachable

A sketch by war artist Dame Laura Knight of Sir Norman Birkett, KC.

seniority. The decision to bestow this role on Lawrence was partly a reflection of his ability to galvanise consensus and partly because it was thought that it shouldn't be an American, to ensure that the tribunal was understood to be truly international. Lawrence commanded the respect of those across the prosecution teams. Summing up an opinion held by many, Roberts commented that he 'presided over his motley assembly with infinite charm, tact, patience and fairness. No one else could have done what he has. Without him the Trial might have been doomed to shipwreck from the start.'[4] Meanwhile, Colonel Andrew Man, who was one the trial's many spectators wrote, 'I was particularly interested to see Lord Lawrence, whose prestige here and everywhere is tremendous. I was told over a drink last night that his name would produce anything anywhere in the zone...Everyone hangs on his words.'[5]

Lieutenant Roger W Barrett, from Chicago, Officer in Charge of the Document Room at the Nuremberg courthouse, taking out a ledger from the safe where all the original documents to be used as evidence against the Nazi war criminals were kept. Photostatic copies were made of all the documents and Barrett is seen checking the originals during the sorting of the photostats.

NEXT PAGE Ralph Koltai's passes from the trial. The reverse of the pass that allowed him to enter the Palace of Justice has been signed by several of the major prosecutors. Koltai was part of the British administrative team, serving as a translator for Hartley Shawcross. He was another individual who had been forced to flee the Nazis and had come to the UK on the *Kindertransport*. He would go on to achieve acclaim as a theatre designer in later life.

Defending the Defendants

The defendants were able to choose their own defence counsel from an Allied-approved list of potential candidates. Though most of the lawyers on this list had been members of the Nazi party themselves, the Allies decided that this should not be an impediment to their involvement – not least because it would have been virtually impossible to find enough lawyers otherwise given the number who had joined the party. If none of the names on the list were considered acceptable, or if those requested were not prepared to take on the case, it was possible for defendants to request their own lawyer. Such candidates would need to be separately vetted and approved. They would also need to be German, not only because it was believed that German lawyers would offer the accused the best chance for a proper defence, but also because there was no realistic prospect of a lawyer from any of the Allied countries taking the challenge up. The only German lawyers that were explicitly denied to those on trial were their fellow defendants, even though a few were qualified lawyers.

Not all the lawyers requested by the defendants were prepared to accept the task at hand. At one stage concerns about having sufficient professionals in place even led to

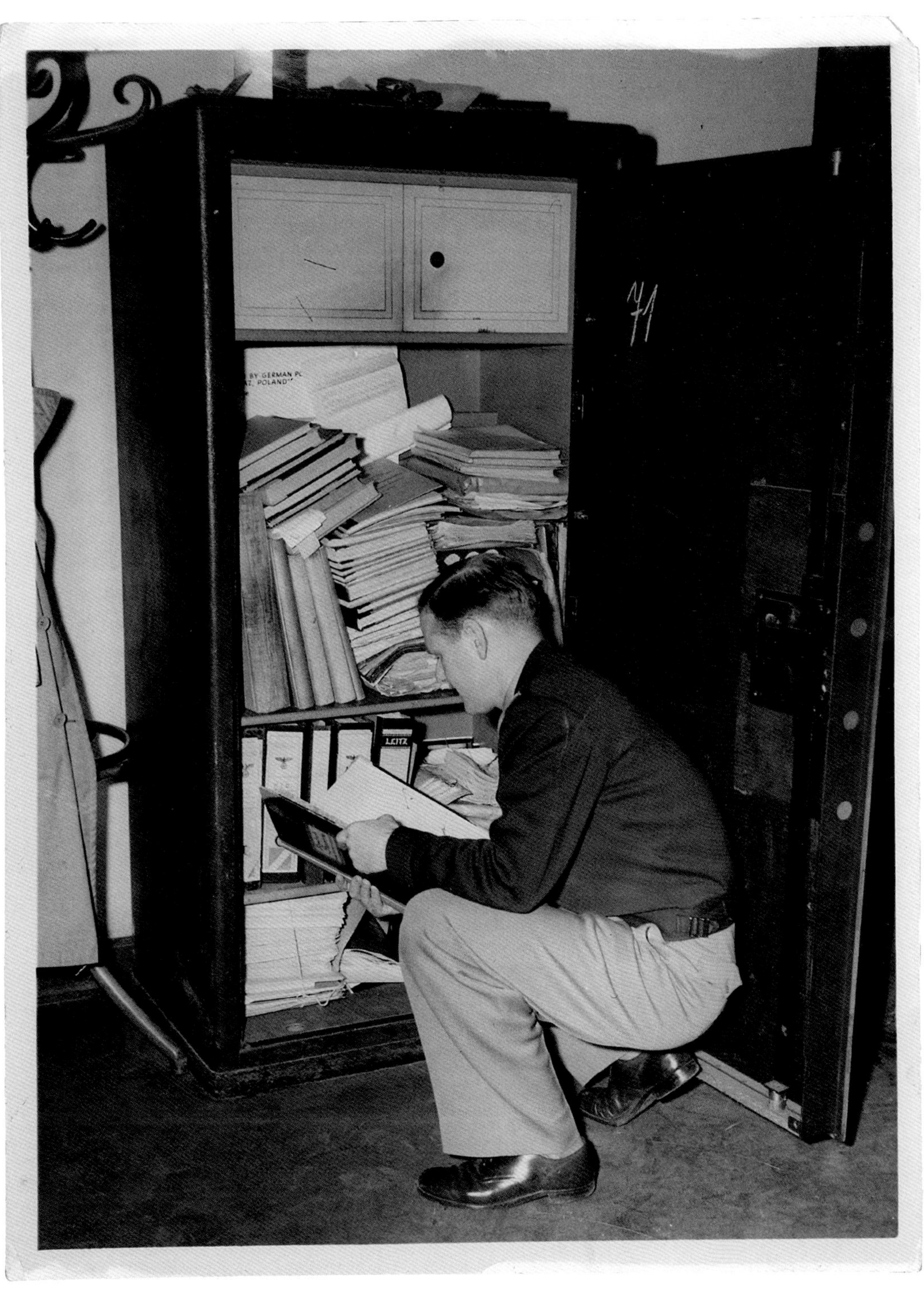

INTERNATIONAL
MILITARY TRIBUNAL
FINAL JUDGEMENT
Session No. 1

BARRIER

Main Court Seat No. 9

1st Half Miss. WILCOX. E. Wilcox
2nd Half Pte. R. KOLTAI. R. Koltai

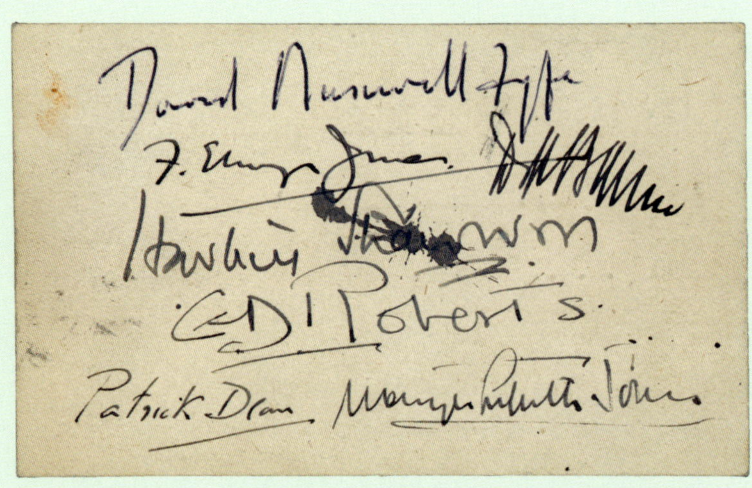

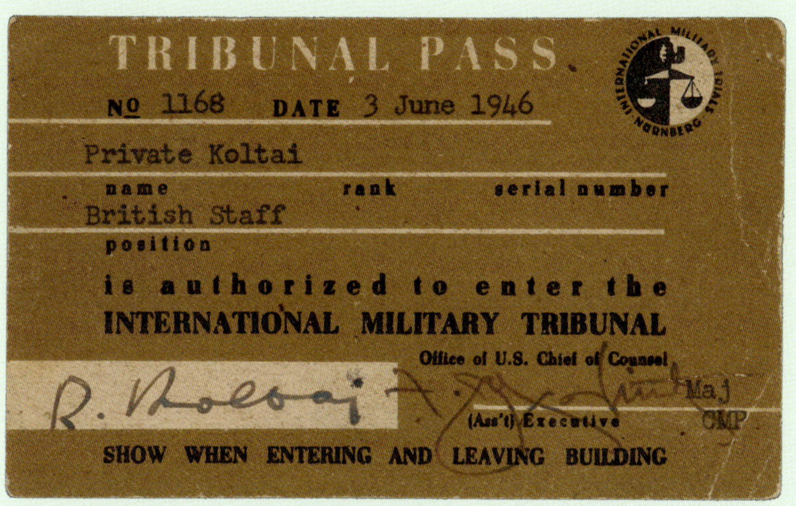

TRIBUNAL PASS

INTERNATIONAL MILITARY TRIALS NÜRNBERG

No 1168 DATE 3 June 1946

Private Koltai

name rank serial number

British Staff

position

is authorized to enter the

INTERNATIONAL MILITARY TRIBUNAL

Office of U.S. Chief of Counsel

R. Koltai

Maj CMP

(Ass't) Executive

SHOW WHEN ENTERING AND LEAVING BUILDING

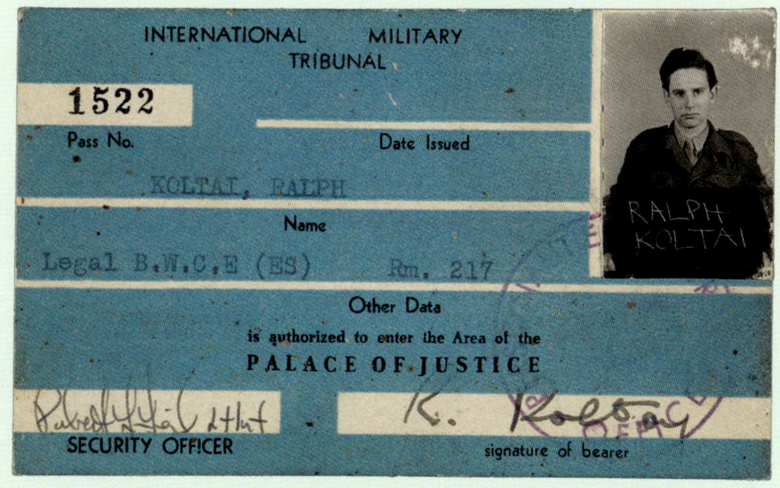

INTERNATIONAL MILITARY TRIBUNAL

1522

Pass No.

Date Issued

KOLTAI, RALPH

Name

RALPH KOLTAI

Legal B.W.C.E (ES) Rm. 217

Other Data

is authorized to enter the Area of the

PALACE OF JUSTICE

SECURITY OFFICER

R. Koltai

signature of bearer

suggestions that those asked should be actively forced to participate – a move ultimately considered unnecessary. The lawyers who did take on the cases did so for a few different reasons. Some undoubtedly felt genuine sympathy for those in the dock and wanted to attempt to help them – Dönitz's counsel, Dr Otto Kranzbühler, for example, was a naval officer and lawyer determined to protect both his client and by extension the reputation of the German Navy more broadly. Others, however, considered it their duty and took the cases not out of sympathy with their clients' politics, but in accordance with their professional obligation to uphold the law. Regardless of their motivations, all were no doubt grateful for the remuneration and the food and Allied rations – such as soap, chocolate, cigarettes and razor blades – it gave them access to.

Such was the judges' determination to proceed entirely properly, at a late stage the anticipated opening date of the trial was pushed back to ensure the defendants had at least 30 days of access to their counsel beforehand. The judges were determined that the defendants be afforded proper process, believing that anything less than these 30 days would have undermined their rights. As per the standard conventions of the judicial system in the West, defence lawyers would be entitled to have sight of any evidence that would be submitted against their clients and would be able to call on witnesses. With these provisions in place, it was felt those in the dock had the fairest chance possible of establishing their innocence.

Gathering the Evidence

Preparing the cases against the defendants relied on compiling evidence, but there were disagreements among the Allied teams about exactly what types of evidence should be used. Jackson's experience led him to believe that it was better to rely on documents rather than witnesses, considering that paper evidence was far less vulnerable to cross-examination than people. Echoing similar thoughts, Calvocoressi – who had been a barrister before the war, and unusually was seconded to the trial by the joint chiefs of staff, so worked across the four prosecution teams – later commented 'we intended to convict these people out of their own mouths'.[6]

> [The decision] was to use and rest on documentary evidence to prove every point possible. The argument against this was that documents are dull, the press would not report on them, the trial would become wearisome and would not get across to the people. There was much truth in this position, I must admit. But it seemed to me that witnesses, many of them persecuted and hostile to the Nazis, would always be chargeable with bias, faulty recollection, and even perjury. The documents could not be accused of partiality, forgetfulness, or invention, and would make the sounder foundation, not only for the immediate guidance of the tribunal, but for the ultimate verdict of history. The result was that the tribunal declared, in its judgment, 'The case, therefore, against the defendants rests in a large measure on documents of their own making.'[7]

Though Jackson was not alone in his conviction about the primacy of documents-based evidence, others felt that the tribunal would need to do something to give the legacy of the crimes a human face. They were concerned that without this, the proceedings could lose the emotional dimension that would be necessary to secure convictions. In the end, Jackson's perspective won out and few witnesses were called to take the stand.

It's important to note that while the tribunal made frequent references to the Nazis' targeting of Jews, this was never separated out from the overall history in a meaningful way due to the way that the case was prepared. Very few of the witnesses were individuals who had been persecuted as Jews either. So, though the defendants were implicitly prosecuted in part for their role in the process of persecution and mass murder of Europe's Jews, they were never pursued for their complicity in the Holocaust specifically.

Sourcing the necessary documentation to form the cases required a considerable and combined effort by the Allies. The Nazis were prodigious record keepers, and they had established a significant paper trail charting their crimes.

In the latter part of the war, realising that these documents were potentially incriminating, they had embarked on efforts to destroy as many of them as possible. Columns of smoke started to appear from offices and concentration camps across the Reich in its final weeks and months. Alice Ehrmann, who was incarcerated in the Theresienstadt ghetto, recorded how 'thousands of pages of documents flew up in flames... the numbers, digits, dates, and names of which our misery is composed... flicker dully and turn to ashes'.[8] The Nazis were sometimes inadvertently assisted in this by the intensification of the Allied bombing campaign, which laid waste to reams of documentation alongside buildings and infrastructure.

However, despite the volume of what had been lost, the sheer amount of paperwork generated by the Nazis also meant that a great deal remained. In the end, it was not too few documents that became the problem but too many. A contemporary observer commented, 'it seems to me utterly unbelievable that the Germans were such congenital fools as to leave such a mass of evidence behind them'[9] – and all this evidence needed to be collected and accounted for. In the final months of the war and in its aftermath teams of Allied personnel swept through former Nazi administrative buildings gathering and collating paperwork. Once secured, librarians and archivists assembled the papers into the necessary systems in order for them to be accessible and usable.

As Calvocoressi commented, 'In the event, we had far more documentation than we had bargained for... but the very fact you had this documentation meant you had to be pretty expert in picking your way through it'.[10]

According to Jackson's analysis, ultimately 100,000 captured documents were screened, of which 10,000 were selected for intensive examination and 4,000 were translated into 4 languages and used in whole, or in part, in the trial. In addition to this, millions of feet of captured film reel were inspected, 100,000 feet of which was bought to Nuremberg. Around 25,000 photographs were also seized, with approximately 1,800 selected and used in the proceedings. Once identified, all this evidence was housed in administrative parts of the estate at Nuremberg.

By the time of the tribunal's completion, the combined

Abraham Sutzkever in the witness stand at the IMT. He remained on his feet throughout as an acknowledgment of the relationship between his testimony and the murder of his child.

efforts of the prosecution teams had resulted in the creation of 30,000 photostats and the production of 50 million typed pages of reports, translated documents and other related paperwork. Even with this volume of evidence, those working for the prosecution teams still had to deal with the ongoing frustration of uncovering items that would have been perfect for elements of the case, only discovered after it was too late for them to be used.

Hedy Epstein, another translator at Nuremberg who had come to Britain on the *Kindertransport*, was part of a team that worked through the captured German documents. She and her colleagues would read the originals and offer a short precis in English of what they contained. If lawyers from the prosecution team thought that the contents looked sufficiently relevant or significant, they would then commission a full translation. Hedy worked from Berlin for most of the time in a documents centre that was deep underground. She described how the US Army colonel in charge of her team was antisemitic and hated the Jewish people working for him – most of whom were refugees from Germany, like Hedy. The situation became so bad that they reported his maltreatment to the Nuremberg authorities, but were told that there was nothing that could be done as he was from the US Army and Nuremberg was managed by the US War Department. She and her colleagues even suspected that he was responsible for some incriminating documents disappearing, though this was never proved.

Witnesses

The witnesses were a broad spectrum of individuals who had seen and experienced the war from very different perspectives. If the number called by the prosecution – 33 – was relatively low, their impact was considerable. Some were men who had blood on their hands themselves, and would eventually be forced to answer for their actions at future national trials, while others had lost virtually everything at the hands of the Nazi regime. Among the former, the testimony of Dr Otto Ohlendorf had a particularly marked impact. Ohlendorf had commanded one of the *Einsatzgruppen* squads that had been responsible for mass murder in Eastern Europe. His testimony formed part of the case against Kaltenbrunner. The dispassionate way in which he relayed the details of the massacres he had overseen had a chilling impact on the court.

Abraham Sutzkever was one of three Jewish witnesses at the IMT. He was a Yiddish poet living in Vilna, Lithuania, when the war broke out. Along with most Jews in the area, he was sent into the city's ghetto with his wife, Freydke, after the Nazis took control. While in the ghetto Freydke gave birth to their first child. Tragically the newborn baby was murdered shortly afterwards. This loss was compounded when Abraham's mother Rayne – who had also been forced to live in the ghetto – was included in a group taken to the Ponary forest and shot. Abraham and Freydke managed to escape from the ghetto in 1943. They joined the partisans and remained with them until the end of the war. Abraham asked if he could give his testimony at Nuremberg in Yiddish, but this request was refused as it wasn't one of the trial's designated languages, so he delivered it in Russian instead. Under questioning from Soviet counsel Smirnov, he described how his son had been killed by a German, while his wife was powerlessly watching. He also relayed the circumstances of his mother's death. He chose to stand throughout his testimony, considering his words a form of *Kaddish* for his murdered child.

CHAPTER FIVE

Recording and Reporting the Trial

Seen through the door of the press work room, working among a litter of hastily thrown aside hats and coats, is Marian Podkowiński of the Polish press, busily putting his copy together.

One of the defining goals of the Nuremberg trial was not only to serve justice but to preserve an unflinching record of the crimes committed by the Nazi regime. As Justice Jackson explained, 'We must let the people of all countries know what has been going on here in Germany if the Nuremberg trials are to accomplish anything for the future peace of the world.'[1] In pursuit of this mission, the trial was documented with an unprecedented fusion of traditional and modern media. Court stenographers produced a verbatim record of every word said, while a parallel audio recording of the proceedings – captured in all four official languages – was pressed on to 750 gramophone records. Photographs were taken by American and British military cameramen, while the US Army Signal Corps captured parts of the proceedings on film. Architect Daniel Kiley, tasked with adapting the courtroom to its new function, incorporated a film screen, a camera platform in a corner of the courtroom and elevated booths to accommodate radio reporters, cameramen and sound engineers recording the trial. The presence of cameras in the courtroom marked a radical departure from legal tradition. While the Soviets had filmed trials before the war, both the British and American legal systems had prohibited cameras in courtrooms. Photos and films were also shown beyond the courtroom.

Journalists for newspapers and radio correspondents were

also permitted to attend and were even encouraged by the trial's organisers. In keeping with the trial's spirit of fairness and openness, Justice Jackson announced that, 'the trial will be completely published. Photo stats of all vital documents will be given to the press immediately upon use'.[2]

During peacetime, journalists covering a trial of such magnitude would have been expected to arrange and fund their own accommodation. But in post-war Nuremberg, such expectations were difficult to meet. Much of the city had been destroyed by the war, and there were few places to stay. The Grand Hotel – one of the last few intact buildings – was already occupied by the trial's legal teams and administrators. To accommodate the press, the Americans hosted around 200 reporters at the Schloss Stein, a grand palace just outside Nuremberg. The reporters were provided with meals and daily transport to the court by jeep. The castle had generous rooms, one of which housed a bar, which fuelled the socialising and partying that was largely funded, or at least 'subbed', by the Americans. The RAF war artist Julius Stafford-Baker late reflected on the trial's remarkable scale and the diversity of the press corps at Nuremberg. He also remembered the atmosphere, noting that drinking was commonplace, with many people 'half-cut' during the day. Baker tried to moderate his drinking as he found he couldn't 'drink and draw'[3].

'The Greatest Trial of All Time', 'The Biggest Murder Trial in History' and other grandiose statements were used in the press to frame the trial at Nuremberg in dramatic terms – partly to sustain public interest in, at times, the slow and dry proceedings. Yet despite concerns about its dullness, the trial attracted no shortage of press interest. By August 1946, the highest number of journalists present at one time had been 235, representing 24 different nations. And it wasn't just reporters who attended: 7,200 official passes – with photographs – had been issued, alongside 7,600 temporary passes.

In this golden age of journalism, some of the most famous writers of the era reported on the trial, including the novelist Rebecca West, William Wyler – who later wrote a much-respected history of the Allied campaign – and the future West German Chancellor Willy Brandt. In Britain, nearly all the national newspapers sent correspondents to Nuremberg.

A general view of the press benches in the courtroom, where the press representatives of many nations listened to the case for the prosecution being presented.

Norman Clark of the *News Chronicle*, who had also attended the Belsen trial, was present, alongside Mea Allan, from the *Daily Herald*, the first woman correspondent to be permanently accredited to the British forces. Both Nicholas Carroll, who wrote for *The Sunday Times*, and the press agency Reuters' war correspondent, Seaghan Maynes, covered the trial from start to finish. Maynes had followed the Allied fighting from Normandy, including a spell with General Patton, and was now sitting only five or six yards away from the defendants. He recorded the proceedings in shifts, passing over to a colleague and then returned to his office to transcribe his notes on a typewriter. From there, it was sent back to London – often in fierce competition with rival press agencies, all racing to file the story first. While Maynes's reports often appeared in local newspapers, local reporters were also sent to cover Nuremberg. A reporter based in Croydon secured one of only two seats allocated to the British press to witness the executions.

After the fall of the Nazi regime, controlling the German press became an important part of the Allies' efforts to reshape public opinion and support the wider aims of the trial. Nazi era newspapers were dissolved and replaced by Allied-backed news sheets and newspapers. While these papers were printed in Germany and staffed by German editors, they were closely supervised. In the British zone, for example, it was reported that editions were flown back to the Foreign Office for censorship.

The plan was to eventually hand control back to German-run, 'anti-Nazi' newspapers. However, by the start of the trial, this shift had only begun to materialise in the Soviet and American zones. In the latter, the *Frankfurter Rundschau* became the first licensed paper, launching on 1 August 1945. By the end of November, there were 18 such publications in circulation. The British zone lagged behind, with its first independent German paper, the *Braunschweiger Zeitung*, not receiving its licence until January 1946. By the close of 1945, the British zone supported 13 newspapers and 5 news sheets, each published twice a week. With circulations ranging from 30,000–60,000 copies, these publications reached a potential readership of 4.5 million.

As the British military prioritised German press coverage

of the proceedings, authorities ensured that German newspapers were well-resourced to report on the trial. At the start of the proceedings, Berlin-based newspapers were given extra paper to ensure they could publish the full text of the indictment[4]. The level of support given to the Berlin-based newspapers didn't go unnoticed. By May 1946, some British journalists began to voice their frustrations, pointing out that while newsprint rationing was limiting its coverage of the proceedings and other political events in Britain, the German media appeared to be receiving preferential treatment. One outlet remarked that: 'Although we here in Britain hear relatively only a small part of the proceedings, it is otherwise in Germany, where the press and radio give them a very wide publicity.'[5] Tensions rose further when five seats originally allocated to British press were reallocated to German reporters for the final judgment[6]. The Allied authorities were determined to ensure the trial's messages reached the German public. One of their more direct efforts was a policy requiring daily classroom discussions about the trial in German schools for pupils between the ages of 12 and 18.

The Press Coverage

As the trial progressed, press interest began to wane, particularly during the prosecution's case. The decision to rely heavily on documentary evidence stifled the opportunities for dramatic exchanges between defendants, witnesses and lawyers. The tone was set from the very first day. One journalist described the scene:

> The proceedings became so dull during the afternoon that dozens of journalists tried to 'escape' from the court room but the guards would permit nobody to leave. Even the judges were at times obviously weary as the reading of the indictment went on alternatively in English, French and Russian. It was almost an endurance test.[7]

Despite these challenges, the trial's organisers were largely satisfied with the coverage. Justice Jackson and Maxwell Fyfe praised the journalists for their 'skilful and fair' reports.[8]

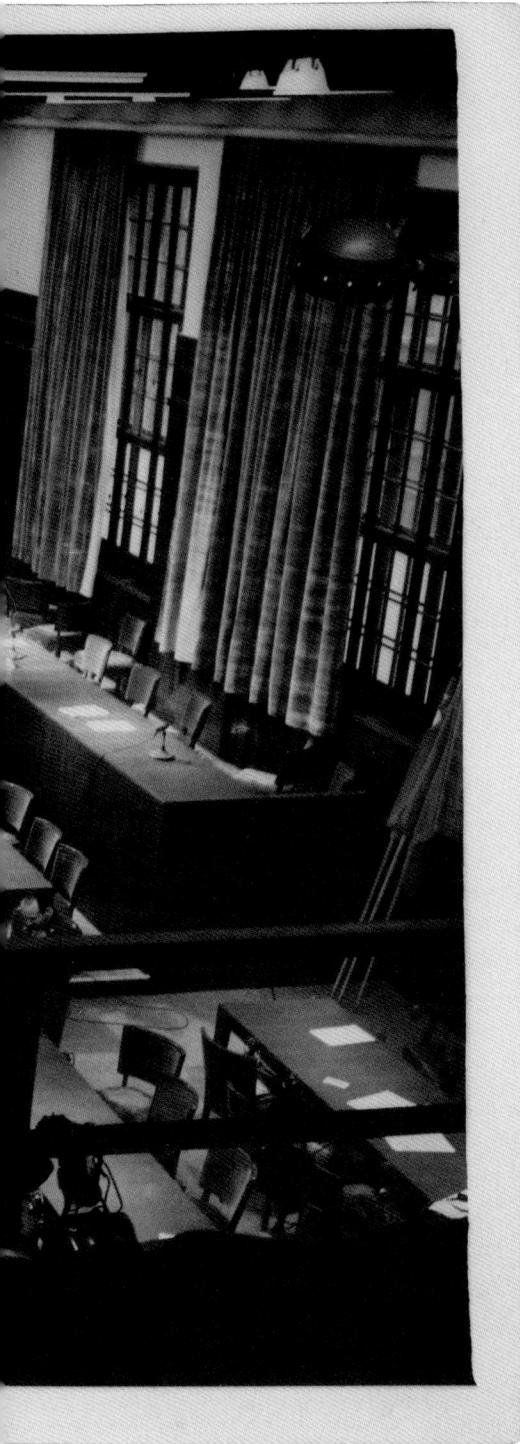

General view of the courtroom at the Palace of Justice. On the far back wall is the projector screen. On the left is the prisoner dock, directly facing them on the right side are the judges' desks. To the right of the screen is the witness box.

Towards the end of the trial, one newspaper compared the coverage of the proceedings across three newspapers – the *Telegraph*, *Manchester Guardian* and *Daily Worker* – with very different political alignments and concluded that the public had been well served by the press. While providing accurate and faithful precis of the proceedings, the journalists also brought the courtroom to life. Their reports added atmosphere and drama that were absent from the official transcripts – details which have proved extremely useful to writers and historians in capturing the true essence of the trial.

Now, much of the press coverage could be seen as sensationalist and simplistic, particularly in its treatment of the Holocaust. The specific targeting of the Jews by the Nazi regime was overlooked and their suffering described in vague, universal terms. Key facts about the exterminating role of Auschwitz-Birkenau and the the other death camps in Nazi-occupied Poland, like Sobibor, were not adequately explored. In some cases, journalists repeated statistics and details without proper care and verification, leading to inaccuracies.[9]

Lights go down during the screening of a film during a session at the trials. Hermann Göring, Walther Funk and Hjalmar Schacht watch intently while Julius Streicher bows his head.

Film at Nuremberg

One of the more distinctive features of the Nuremberg trial was the use of film – not only to document the proceedings, but also as part of the evidence screened in court. While filming war crimes trials was still a relatively new idea, it wasn't entirely unprecedented. In 1943, the Soviet Union had recorded parts of the trials held in Krasnodar (14–17 July 1943) and Kharkov (15–18 December 1943). Though the proceedings were not fully recorded, footage from both trials was later used in propaganda films, including a Soviet newsreel on Krasnodar and a full-length documentary from Kharkov titled *Justice is Coming*, which was released internationally in 1944. The British had also experimented with filming trials. In the autumn of 1944, they arranged for the trials of the two notorious Italian collaborators, Pietro Caruso and Vincenzo Azzolini, to be filmed. Clips from these were shared with both Italian and British newsreels.

At Nuremberg, the filming was more limited. Only 54 hours of footage were recorded, capturing just the key moments, such

6N

as the opening and closing statements, the defendants' pleas and the sentencing, in full. Outside of these sessions, filming was restricted to just two hours per day, as there were concerns that the continual presence of cameras might disrupt the proceedings.

While propaganda had been the driving force behind the filming of earlier war crimes trials in the Soviet Union and Italy, the approach at Nuremberg was notably different – at least in its planning stages. Here, the intention was not solely to influence public opinion, but to create a lasting historical record. The filming was the concluding element of the American 'War Crimes Photographic Project', which aimed to 'compile a motion picture record of great historical value to the United States Government.'[10]

Beyond serving as a historical record, the filmed proceedings soon came to be seen as a powerful tool of propaganda for the occupying powers. Publicising the crimes of the Nazi regime through courtroom footage helped to weaken any lingering support for the old order, while also presenting the Allied occupation as one grounded in justice and the rule of law. The Allied war crimes trials featured prominently in *Welt im Film*, a German-language newsreel series produced jointly by the British and Americans to replace the Nazi-era *Die Deutsche Wochenschau.* Footage from the IMT was also distributed to Allied newsreels beyond Germany, helping to justify the war and its suffering by presenting audiences with the scale of Nazi criminality.

Plans were also made to produce a special Allied documentary that would summarise the trial and its findings – a kind of cinematic final reckoning of the Nazi regime. The idea combined footage of the proceedings with captured German film to create a powerful visual account. As Sandra Schulberg, the daughter of Stuart Schulberg who worked on the project, explained, the film had two main goals: 'to demonstrate to the world the essential fairness of the Nuremberg trial and to show to the German people what atrocities their Nazi leaders had committed.'[11] Eventually, the concept evolved into two separate films. The Soviet Union released *Sud Narodov (Judgment of the Peoples)* in 1947, while the American production, *Nürnberg und Seine Lehre* (*Nuremberg: Its Lesson for Today*), was released in Germany in 1948.

A still from *The Nazi Plan* – a compilation of German footage covering the history of the Third Reich used as prosecution evidence at the trials. Hess, outside the Party Building in Munich's Königsplatz, with Ley and von Schirach behind, leads an assembled gathering in oath to Hitler.

Today, the footage of the trial offers moments of drama and interactions that the official transcript cannot fully capture. It reveals the reactions and expressions of those in the dock and the witness box, as well as their demeanour under cross-examination. For some observers these visual cues were more telling than the words themselves. The footage also conveys the slow, methodical pace of the proceedings. Scenes of towering documents, and the steady actions of the diligent court staff, reflect its complexity and admirable air of thoroughness.

Film as Evidence

The film evidence at Nuremberg fell into two categories. The first consisted of footage, shot by combat and newsreel cameramen who had accompanied the armies of the western Allies and the Red Army. This footage recorded the aftermath of Nazi atrocities and showed scenes of concentration camps, POW and labour camps, as well as the destruction of towns, national monuments and artefacts across occupied Europe.

The second category was captured German footage. Under the policy of *Gleichschaltung* (coordination), the Nazi regime had brought all film production, distribution and screening in Germany under state control. Overseen by Propaganda Minister Joseph Goebbels, the regime produced a vast number of films, ranging from harmless entertainment to overt propaganda. Some, like *Triumph of the Will* (1935), were already notorious to the Allies. Of the 1,094 feature films and 2,500 short films seized and reviewed by the Allies, 141 features and 245 short films were later categorised as 'Forbidden'.

As with the captured documents and records, the Allies believed that that films could serve as vital evidence of Nazi crimes. In the summer and autumn of 1945, the OSS Field Photographic Branch was established to locate and assess Nazi film footage. The hunt began in the US, where useful material was found in German newsreels held by the Fox Movietone News collection, at the Museum of Modern Art, and among films held by the German-American community in New York. A key figure in the search was Dr Karl Jacoby, a former Berlin prosecutor who had fled to the US in 1941. A committed anti-Nazi, Jacoby identified numerous incriminating scenes for the prosecution.

A parallel search was also underway in Germany. Large collections of film were retrieved from the personal archive of official Nazi photographer Heinrich Hoffmann,[12] where millions of feet of sound documentaries and 1,200 film stills were held, as well as from collections in Bayreuth and Rodersdorf, east of Berlin. In some cases, however, the Allied operatives arrived too late – finding only smouldering piles of film cans, likely destroyed after tip-offs to their German custodians. To assist with the interpretation and editing of the footage, American editors worked alongside German experts, including Jacoby and several Nazi film technicians. Among them were Hoffmann himself, editors Walter Rode and Kurt von Molo and director Leni Riefenstahl, who was subpoenaed to assist and spent three months in Nuremberg working on the project.

The screening of *Nazi Concentration Camps* on 29 November 1945 – the eighth day of the Nuremberg trial – is often considered the first use of film evidence at a war crimes court. However, a few months earlier, on 20 September, during the fourth day of the Belsen trial, British prosecutors had already introduced film as evidence. The 21-minute *Belsen Camp Evidence Film*, compiled by the Judge Advocate General from British Army footage taken shortly after the camp's liberation, was shown in court as a kind of cinematic witness for the prosecution. The film included scenes that had previously been censored by the War Office and had a profound impact on those present and was widely referred to in the press. Encouraged by the response, the prosecution later introduced an official Soviet documentary film on Auschwitz, further establishing the role of film as compelling evidence.

The screenings at the Belsen trial were significant not only for their immediate impact, but also for the precedent they set. They established a legal and practical framework for the use of film as courtroom evidence – an approach that would later be adopted and expanded at the IMT. Building on this model, the planners of the IMT undertook a far more ambitious use of film, screening a total of ten films across of a wide range of genres, including amateur footage, documentaries, newsreels, propaganda films and official combat recordings.[13]

The innovative use of film as evidence was only made

possible by special provisions in the Allied war crimes legislation. Regulation 8(i) of the Royal Warrant and Article 19 of the Charter of the Tribunal relaxed the usual rules of evidence, allowing judges to admit material based on its probative value rather strict legal standards. This meant that affidavits and film – forms of evidence that might otherwise have been excluded – could be accepted in court.

All of the films shown during the trial were presented as evidence for the prosecution, with all but two screened during the prosecution's phase of the proceedings. In the lead up to the trial, there were detailed discussions about how and when each film should be shown. Commander James Donovan, for example, recommended that *Nazi Concentration Camps* be screened during the section on this topic, while the *Trial of July 20 Plotters* was proposed for use in the case against Hans Frank. However, the prosecution was not averse to running films out of sequence for tactical reasons. Donovan even suggested that '... if at any time the defence counsel get out of hand and are complaining about the entire proceeding, we offer to show the Tribunal the Nazi courts in operation.'[14]

When films were shown according to the programme, the prosecutors typically screened them after presenting documentary evidence and hearing witness testimony. In their view, the films served as a powerful way to visualise the material already introduced and to reinforce the case in a memorable form. However, in the case of *Nazi Concentration Camps*, Donovan *recommended* that it be shown at the very start of the concentration camp case. Film was seen as particularly effective in conveying the scale and horror of the atrocities – scenes that even those behind the camera struggled to describe. Sergeant William Lawrie, who filmed at Bergen-Belsen, later admitted that 'words are quite inadequate to describe the terrible scenes he witnessed in the camp'.[15] When introducing *Nazi Concentration Camps*, US Prosecutor J T Dodd explained:

> If it pleases the Tribunal, the Prosecution for the United States will at this time present to the Tribunal, with its permission, a documentary film on concentration camps. This is by no means the entire proof which the prosecution will offer with respect to the subject of concentration

The top still is a shot from reel 1 of the British film, *The Belsen Camp Evidence Film* (1945).

The bottom still is a shot from reel 2 of *Nazi Concentration Camps* (1945) and shows Buchenwald concentration camp after its liberation by the US Forces.

camps, but this film which we offer represents in a brief and unforgettable form an explanation of what the words 'concentration camp' imply.[16]

Film also served to make tangible the destruction described in verbal testimony or documentary evidence, particularly in relation to the devastation of towns and buildings of historical or cultural value. One striking example was the Soviet documentary *Destruction Perpetrated by the Germans on the Territories of the Soviet Union.*

Nuremberg Trial: Seen from the BBC recording window high above the back of the International Military Tribunal – two Russian judges, two British, two American and two French by Julius Stafford-Baker.

Legal Procedure

Each film screening at the trial was accompanied by a degree of legal formality to ensure its admissibility as evidence. Typically, this involved an affidavit presented to the tribunal to establish the provenance of the film – who had created, discovered, or compiled it – and its authenticity as either an original or authentic copy. The affidavit also included the exhibit number assigned to the film, which was read out in court as part of the official record.

Prosecuting lawyers often prefaced the screening with apologies for technical imperfections – footage that was too short, poorly shot, or scratched. These acknowledgements prepared the court for the technical limitations of the material and, ironically, elevated the footage's evidentiary value by highlighting that the films were fragile originals – documentaries of crimes that were captured as they were being committed.

The Significance of Film Evidence

The use of captured German films in the trial of the Nazi leadership carried a symbolic weight not unlike the decision to hold the proceedings in Nuremberg – a city so closely associated with the Nazi regime. Given the notorious role of propaganda in sustaining the Nazi era, it seemed fitting that the Allies should use it against the regime's leading men. 'We will show you their own films'[17], declared Jackson in his opening address, signalling the prosecution's intent to let the

Nazis condemn themselves. The irony of screening German propaganda at a trial to convict its creators was not lost on members of the prosecution. Roberts KC, who cross-examined Alfred Jodl, noted:

> German documentary films – showing the rise and fall of the Nazi party. Göring and all the other defendants making speeches... Condemning themselves out of their own mouths. These ought to be good. There is one of Göring goose-stepping which may test the gravity of the Tribunal[18]

Captured German footage was just one category among several types of film evidence presented at the trial. These were shown either in their original form or edited into new compilations. The range included:

- **Allied footage** documenting German war crimes, typically filmed in the aftermath by newsreel and combat cameramen. These reels were mostly unedited, silent and accompanied by shot sheets.

- **Amateur footage,** often shot anonymously, but believed to have been filmed by German military personnel.

- ***Die Deutsche Wochenschau*****,** the official Nazi-era newsreel series, accompanied by music, narration and sound effects.

- **German official propaganda films,** both short and feature-length, produced under state direction and often ideological.

- **German military training and documentary films,** used for internal instruction and public messaging.

- **Allied documentary compilations,** such as *Nazi Concentration Camps* (1945), constructed mainly from Allied footage and accompanied by live and recorded commentary.

- ***The Nazi Plan* (1945),** an American-produced archival montage that wove together captured German footage with explanatory English intertitles to present a chronological narrative of the Nazi regime.

The legal use of film evidence at the trial served a range of purposes, each carefully considered by the prosecution. These functions fell into six categories:

- **Identifying offenders:** In the lead-up to the trial, US prosecutors used captured German footage, such as films of Nazi Party rallies, to identify leading Nazis and to implicate the accused. In one notable instance, Rudolf Hess was brought into a cutting room and shown footage of himself addressing the 1934 Nuremberg rally in *Triumph of the Will* (1935) to challenge his claims of amnesia.[19]

- **Direct evidence of crimes:** Some German-made films, captured by the Allies, documented atrocities as they occurred. These included *Atrocities Against Jews*, which showed the 'extermination of a ghetto', and *Destruction of Lidice* (1942), which recorded the destruction of a Czech town as a reprisal for the assassination of Reich Protector Reinhard Heydrich. According to US prosecutor Commander Donovan, *Atrocities Against Jews* offered 'undeniable evidence, made by Germans themselves, of almost incredible brutality to Jewish people in the custody of the Nazis including German military units.'[20]

- **Crime scene documentation:** Allied documentaries, such as the American film *Nazi Concentration Camps* and the Soviet production *Film Documents of the Atrocities Committed by the German Fascist Invaders* (1946), provided visual context for witness testimony. These films, compiled by footage shot by military cameramen during the liberation of the camps, were essential in conveying the scale of the crimes – especially as many camps had been tidied up and sanitised by the start of the trial, and all the documentation of the camps had been destroyed by the Germans. It was difficult to convey the dreadful conditions, but the bodies of the victims were the evidence. The films showed corpses, the emaciated survivors, looted belongings, the physical infrastructure of the camps, including barbed wire, watchtowers and instruments of torture and murder. Their structure often followed a site-by-site format – and while they were assembled quickly, in months, and sometimes re-edited from military reports – they relied heavily on the information in the cameramen's shot sheets and any military intelligence that had been gathered. As there was not a complete understanding at the time of the full scope of the Nazi crimes, these films occasionally contained inaccuracies and were also coloured by contemporary political attitudes, including a tendency to universalise the suffering of the Nazis' victims. The films failed to acknowledge that Jews were the people most persecuted by the Nazi regime.

- **Authenticating testimony:** Some films included statements from witnesses. In *Nazi Concentration Camps*, for example, US Serviceman Lieutenant Jack Taylor, who had been liberated from Mauthausen, and Dr Hadassah Bimko, from Belsen, described their treatment and the conditions at the camps, with the film footage providing a corroborative backdrop to their testimony.

- **Narrative construction:** The Allied compilation *The Nazi Plan* used German newsreels and propaganda films to chart a chronological account of the Nazi regime's rise and crimes.

- **Incriminating defendants:** Films were also used tactically during cross-examination. *Hitler's Triumphant Return to Berlin*, shown on 3 May

1946, showed Hjalmar Schacht effusively shaking Hitler's hand – undermining his claims of distance from the regime. Similarly, *Reichsbank Loot*, screened on 7 May 1946, contradicted Walther Funk's defence that the bank's vault did not hold cash and valuables stolen from prisoners of concentration camps.

× **Tactical programming:** Beyond their evidentiary value, the films were used to stimulate interest in the proceedings. The screening of the first film, *Nazi Concentration Camps*, was brought forward to revive waning press interest in the trial. Other films, such as those showing the intimidation of defendants in the *Trial of 20 July Plotters* (1945), were screened to undermine the morale of the defendants.

The Limitations

The value of the films shown at Nuremberg as legal evidence has since come under scrutiny. One key criticism is that the footage did not depict the defendants themselves, or crimes directly committed by them. Instead, the films often presented broader scenes of atrocity, leaving a gap between the evidence and individual accountability. There were also factual inaccuracies, particularly in the Allied-produced documentaries. For example, *Nazi Concentration Camps* includes footage of British prisoners of war at Fallingbostel, mistakenly identified in the commentary as prisoners at Belsen. This error likely stemmed from the rushed nature of the film's production and the unfamiliarity of American editors with footage shot by the British Army Film Unit. There are also concerns around how the films were used. Since they couldn't be questioned like a witness, it made them less reliable than live testimony. Alongside these technical complaints, some now believe the films of the concentration camps and atrocities weren't really used as solid legal evidence, but more to deliver a form of retribution and to publicly put the German nation on trial.[21]

Another issue was the way the footage was selected and edited. *Nazi Concentration Camps* makes no reference to the Holocaust, or the targeted genocide of Jews, Sinti and Roma, and barely mentions Jewish suffering. In light of these gaps and errors, such films would likely need careful editing and explanation if they were used as evidence in a modern war crimes trial. Still, at the time, these issues and errors did not invalidate the films. They were made in good faith, using real, documented footage, and with a sincere attempt to make a new form of evidence valid. Under the Nuremberg Charter, it was up to the judges to assess the probative value of all evidence, and by those standards, the films were seen as valid and important.

A film still from *Nazi Concentration Camps* showing one of around 70 women prisoners who were liberated by the US forces from Penig concentration camp on 17 April 1945.

A shot of Dachau concentration camp, taken from reel 2 of *Nazi Concentration Camps*.

CHAPTER SIX

The Artists' Coverage

A preliminary sketch for Laura Knight's *The Nuremberg Trial.*

Alongside the modern technology used to record the trial, artists were also present, capturing the proceedings in a way that added a deeper emotional dimension to the coverage. These artists offered unique interpretations of moments that were difficult to convey by camera, like the expressions of the accused as they watched film evidence unfold in court. Captain Bryan de Grineau's sketches, drawn during the screening of the American film *Nazi Concentration Camps,* are a striking example, capturing the moment footage of the mass graves at Bergen-Belsen were shown at the trial (see pages 98–99). The scene no doubt resonated with de Grineau, who had visited the camp himself to create drawings for the *Illustrated London News* and *The Sphere.* De Grineau's drawing illustrated a dramatic moment in the trial, very much in the tradition of law court artists in the era before photography. Other artists, such as Dame Laura Knight, whose painting *The Nuremberg Trial* is discussed later, were less interested in creating a snapshot of the trial, much like a photographer, but in conveying its deeper meaning through the impressions and sketches she developed over many visits to the court. While some artists strove to create neutral, objective pictures, more fitting to the legal process, others, such as the caricaturists, pictured the accused as evil men to be ridiculed and lampooned.

GALLOWS
WITHIN SLEEPING QUARTERS AT LEAST TWO THIRDS EITHER DEAD OR DYING
PILE OF OLD REMNANTS OF BOOTS TAKEN FROM PREVIOUS DEAD INMATES. INERT FIGURES CROUCHED AROUND
43
WOMAN SLOWLY MOVING WITH BOWL OF WATER –
WOMEN MAKING FEEBLE LITTLE FIRES OF RAGS SITTING AMONG BODIES
EXTERMINATION BY STARVATION – THIRST AND DESEASE –
DRAWN IN
ONE OF THE WOMENS SECTIONS WHOSE INMATES WERE JUST
LIVING-DEAD, EXISTING AMIDST THE DEAD. HERE WERE MEN, WOMEN
AND CHILDREN – IMPOSSIBLE TO TELL WHO STILL BREATHED AMONG THE BODIES LYING AROUND
THOSE LIVING QUITE INDIFFERENT TO SURROUNDINGS. THE FEARFUL STENCH – THE CLOUDS
OF DESEASE-INFECTED DUST – THE COMPLETE CESSATION OF ALL DECENCY OF
HUMAN BEINGS REDUCED TO ANIMALS AND EVEN TO CANNIBALISM
IT IS IMPOSSIBLE TO PORTRAY
29. Belsen Death Camp

Bryan de Grineau's sketch, *Belsen Concentration camp, Germany.*

A selection of sketched poses of Hermann Göring and Rudolf Hess by David Low at the Nuremberg trials.

Bryan de Grineau's sketch of *Göring sweeping his cell.*

Under the British legal system, sketching and portrait making had been banned in criminal courts since 1925 – though court artists could take notes and sketch from memory later. This was not the case in the US, which helps to explain why artists were allowed to draw during the proceedings. Allowing artists to work in the courtroom broadened the IMT's appeal beyond specialist courtroom illustrators, helping to elevate it as a more significant cultural and historical event.

Art was taken seriously by the trial organisers, particularly as many of the artists were working in an official capacity on behalf of their respective governments. During the trial, artists were located in the visitor's balcony, above the press box, overlooking the prosecutors – often using binoculars to view their subjects closely. The court also made efforts to accommodate individual artists' preferences. Knight, for example, preferred to work in solitude and was given a prime spot in a US radio booth, above the dock, away from the other artists. British IMT Secretary Ian Mcilwraith applied to the judge to allow British war artist Feliks Topolski greater access, noting: 'He would like to sit nearer the defendants. Would you mind if he sat at the end of the table – the Tribunal table – during the 2 days he is here. He has a small discreet sketchbook.'[1]

Perhaps aware of the momentous nature of the trial, Knight found that the lawyers, guards, hotel staff and others took a great deal of interest in her work, and she was given a special room to act as a studio when she began painting her main piece and was asked to exhibit her work at the hotel where she was staying. The accused in the dock also seemed to like the attention of being depicted by the artists.

Many artists, including Feliks Topolski, Joseph Otto Flatter and the political cartoonist David Low, chose to focus on the trial's participants, especially the accused. Low found the war criminals on display a disappointment:

> I recognised the men in the dock instantly...After what had happened, I did not look, of course for a set of puffed-up specimens of the Master Race in fearsome uniforms with padded shoulders, swastikas and high heels; but on the other hand this lot seemed rather inadequate.[2]

B. DE G.

A sketch of Hermann Göring and Rudolf Hess at the Nuremberg trial by Joseph Otto Flatter.

Low also found the prisoners a colourless bunch, reflecting their stressed emotional state: 'If one were painting the historic scene, one would have to use a palette of drab pigments.'[3] His observations on the visual atmosphere of the trial also reflected his impression of the trial as a whole: 'The proceedings in court are prosaic and undramatic while I am there, which is how they should be to my way of thinking.'[4]

Low's pencil sketches of the accused were often captured in a series of poses, drawn from observations made during a session at the trial. Unsurprisingly Göring was the most prominent figure in the courtroom, with Low noting that: 'Göring stands out by a mile as the boss in this company.'[5] He was the most interesting and engaging for many of the artists to observe, especially for Low as a caricaturist:

> He is a restless prisoner, leaning this way and that, flapping his pudgy little hands about, patting his hair, stroking his mouth, massaging his cheeks, resting his chin sideways on the ledge of the dock.[6]

In his completed cartoon of Göring, Low brings together a selection of the sketched poses, depicting him as a frightening calculating force, staring out his adversaries. This depiction is rooted in a personal encounter Low had while at the trial:

> Sketchbook in hand, I am examining Göring meticulously when he turns his gaze and hooks my eye. After about twenty seconds of mutual glaring it dawns upon me that he is trying to stare me down. The childish vanity of it! How silly! (I win, by the way.)[7]

Göring tried to out-stare various people who attended the trial, but on occasion the tables were turned on him by those seeking a small measure of personal revenge on the notorious Nazi leader. One such example was refugee Hedy Epstein, whose parents were murdered at Auschwitz. She worked at the trial as an analyser of captured documents:

During a recess in the Trial I stood in front of Göring. I didn't say anything, I just looked at him...and he was obviously uncomfortable, and he didn't know who I was and I was wearing a uniform, we were given American uniforms, and so he probably didn't even suspect that I would know German, and he said to his German defence counsel, in German, 'Who is this little one, what does she want?' And the defence counsel says, 'I don't know who she is, but she obviously works for the prosecution, and I don't know what she wants but just don't say anything, don't do anything.' And I'm thinking, you know, here is Göring whom not too long ago I would have feared mortally and here I am, and he's afraid of me! Who would believe? And again, but I always came back to this, and I still do sometimes now, little Hedy from Kippenheim and there is Göring and he's afraid of me![8]

The Austrian Jewish painter and cartoonist Joseph Otto Flatter, who had moved to England in 1934, held a personal animus to the men on trial, which he expressed in his anti-Nazi cartoons, notably a popular series satirising Hitler's *Mein Kampf* produced between 1938–1939, prompted by the *Anschluss* and the annexation of Czechoslovakia. Initially Flatter's vehemence against the Nazis did not match the mood in Britain, and some regarded him as a 'war monger', but Flatter recalled that, 'when the bombs started to fall on London the mood change[ed]'.[9] Flatter was called to a Tribunal to 'decide between the black and white sheep' and categorised as a 'Harmless Enemy Alien';[10]nevertheless he was still later interned for two to three months on the Isle of Man. After this episode he was commissioned by the Ministry of Information (MOI) to design propaganda leaflets to frighten the German soldiers who were poised to invade. Flatter continued to receive occasional commissions from the MOI, and it was under these auspices that he travelled to Nuremberg. Flatter was keen to take up the commission and 'see the people I had pilloried during the war, I wanted to see them in the flesh.... but when I saw the accused like small men sitting in two rows I had pity for them'.[11]

Flatter drew many sketches of the accused from the upper gallery, where most of the artists worked, and had to view his subjects through binoculars. He also drew the prisoners in their cells. From these sketches he made larger watercolours of the dock. While he may have felt some pity for the prisoners, the intention of his humiliating drawings of the Nazis was straightforward: 'It was not my ambition to show my artistry. I regarded my drawings as a substitute for bombs and shells, and they had to be hard hitting.'[12]

The Polish Jewish painter and draughtsman Feliks Topolski came to Britain in 1935 to record King George V's Silver Jubilee for a Polish magazine, but stayed once the Nazis invaded Poland. At the start of the war, he worked for the Polish armed forces and later the War Artists Advisory Committee (WAAC) at the MOI. As an official war artist, Topolski travelled widely and covered numerous topics, including the first Arctic convoy to Russia, Britain's home front and the Blitz, as well as the Polish Air Force. His drawings of the trial were one of his last

A series of six cartoons by Joseph Otto Flatter satirising Adolf Hitler's *Mein Kampf*.

MEIN KAMPF

CHAPTER VIII

The Beginning of My Political Activities

One day I put my name down as wishing to take part in the discussion.

Another of the participants thought that he would break a lance for the Jews and entered into a lengthy defence of them.

This aroused my opposition.

An overwhelming number of those who attended the lecture course supported my views.

The consequence of it all was that, a few days later, I was assigned to a regiment then stationed at Munich and given a position there as 'instruction officer'.

FLatter.39

Here again I made the acquaintance of several comrades whose thought ran along the same lines as my own and who later became members of the first group out of which the new movement developed.

official commissions. Topolski's pencil drawing, *The Nuremberg Trial, 1946*, doesn't depict the courtroom itself but focuses on the accused in the dock – portrayed as a single, sinister entity: a band of old gangsters, still dangerous despite their incarceration. The sketch was eventually published in 1960 in the *Chronicle* and titled *Revival*, serving as a warning against the resurgence of fascism to a younger generation.

By contrast, Flight-Lieutenant Julius Stafford-Baker's dispassionate watercolour, *Nuremberg Trial: The Nazi Conspirators Guarded by American Military Police*, offers a greater sense of the trial as a whole, showing the courtroom itself as well as some of the other participants and the accused. Stafford-Baker faithfully records the architecture of the handsome remodelled courtroom, including even obscure details such as the air vents and wall carvings. The defendants

Two benches of the accused leaders stretch across Feliks Topolski's pencil drawing, *The Nuremberg Trial, 1946*. Just in view behind the defendants are the torsos of a line of military police who guard the benches and separate them from the court beyond. In front of the defendants sits a lawyer or clerk in black robes and another figure is seated to the right.

are presented without interpretation, or caricature, with no inkling of the crimes for which they are accused present – if it was not for the presence of the guards, the men depicted could easily be participants in a meeting to discuss urban planning!

Stafford-Baker's companion painting, *Nuremberg, the Trial: A general view of the crowded court when the Nazi conspirators faced the International Military Tribunal*, is similarly undramatic and factual, presenting the trial as a distant event. The painting offers a realistic vision of the trial, capturing the atmosphere as well as the layout. Nearly all the participants, including prosecutor Maxwell Fyfe, have their back to the viewer.

The son of an illustrator and cartoonist, with a brother who was also an artist, Stafford-Baker was immersed in the arts from an early age. When the war began, Stafford-Baker, who was also passionate about planes, joined the RAF, where he

Julius Stafford-Baker's watercolour *Nuremberg Trial: The Nazi Conspirators Guarded by American Military Police*. From left to right the men in the box are Admiral Karl Dönitz (wearing dark glasses), Erich Raeder, Baldur von Schirach, Fritz Sauckel and Alfred Jodl. Hermann Göring is in the front row, with his face half obscured by the back of an American policeman wearing a light-grey uniform. The black hair just above Göring's head belongs to Rudolf Hess. The other five in the box are Hans Frank, Wilhelm Frick, Julius Streicher, Walther Funk and Hjalmar Schacht.

Julius Stafford-Baker's watercolour *Nuremberg, the Trial: A general view of the crowded court when the Nazi conspirators faced the International Military Tribunal*. The judges are seated on the right, with the defendants on the left surrounded by UN guards.

Julius Stafford-Baker's painting, *Nuremberg: All that is left of the commercial centre after heavy raids by the RAF*, shows the destroyed city of Nuremberg after heavy bombing by the RAF.

carried on drawing and painting, making numerous portraits and studies of fellow RAF members and the aircraft they flew. He showed his portfolio to the war artist Stanley Spencer, who secured him an interview with the WAAC, and was soon transferred from military intelligence to the RAF Public Relations Directorate. As an official war artist, Stafford-Baker was able to cover the wider story of the RAF at war, including the fighting in Italy, the defeat of Berlin and eventually the Nuremberg trial, which he attended of his own accord, arriving on 30 December 1945. When the trial was postponed due to a fault with the court's heating system, Stafford-Baker made drawings around the city, recording the impact of the war on local landmarks, like Albrecht Dürer's birthplace. Among this series is a powerful watercolour, unironically titled *Nuremberg: All that is left of the commercial centre after heavy raids by the RAF*. While Stafford-Baker's watercolours of the trial keep the clear, illustrative style of an official record, here he shifts towards commentary. The scene of Nuremberg's destruction is looser and less precise, showing empathy for the vulnerable figures walking below the ruins, overshadowed by the destruction of war.

Despite Stafford-Baker's generally cool and matter of fact style, matching the tone of his interviews about his wartime service, the toll of the war eventually wore him down. He moved to Shetland to recuperate, where he found solace in drawing quiet isolated crofts and fishing villages.

A portrait by Laura Knight of G D Roberts viewed from the side, examining some papers at his desk.

Dame Laura Knight

The first female Royal Academician, Dame Laura Knight had already been working as a war artist for six years by the time she went to Nuremberg to record the trial. A traditional, accessible painter of oils, her wartime works celebrated the contribution of young men and women to the war effort in a manner that borders on the heroic. Alongside her glamorous paintings of aircrew and uniformed women, which could be seen as a continuation of her pre-war paintings of circus performers and the theatre, she also had many commissions to record the war production and the workers on the factory front. Her famous painting of Ruby Loftus became a symbol of

Laura Knight's oil painting *The Nuremberg Trial*. Her painting reproduces faithfully the courtroom scene and is, in effect, a group portrait of the prisoners who are shown wearing the cumbersome headphones necessary to hear a translation of the proceedings.

women's vital contributions to the war effort. She was diligent and willing to take on any official commission, no matter how seemingly drab the topic or uncomfortable the location. Just before Nuremberg, Knight was proud of having stuck out six weeks in a ball-bearing factory.[13] Even so, when invited to paint tank manoeuvres, she asked the WAAC, 'What about the trial at Nuremberg for a subject, instead of tanks?',[14] and flew to Nuremberg on 5 January 1946, returning to England in late April.

By the time of her trip to the trial, Knight had become a celebrity artist, even broadcasting from Nuremberg for the BBC. As a VIP, with a large suite in the Grand Hotel, she ate well and had access to the privileged social life of the trial. The commission was not just an end of term jaunt for Knight; she took her work very seriously, even writing a journal of her time in Nuremberg – the first time she had recorded her work in this way. Compassionate and observant, Knight was very much aware of her privileged status and felt uncomfortable when she saw the destruction of the city and the thin, poorly clothed locals.

During her time in Nuremberg, Knight produced various sketches of the defendants in the dock, which became the basis of the oil painting that she produced in time for the 1946 Royal Academy Summer Show. She also painted a number of portraits, including pastel drawings of the trial's president (judge) Lord Justice Lawrence and of the prosecuting barristers in the British delegation: Maxwell Fyfe, Roberts and Birkett.

The Main Painting

While in Nuremberg, Knight was deeply affected by the destruction that war had left on the city. She also felt compassion for those she met who had lived through the war and wanted to convey this in her painting. As Knight wrote to her husband, who was also an artist, she sought a structural solution that would convey the consequences of the war, which were at the heart of the often dry and formal proceedings of the courtroom. She noted in a letter to her husband, 'I am trying out my rather crazy idea which gives me an opportunity for space and mystery, I do hope so much I can bring it off…I will

not say what the idea is, only that it is not normal.'[15]

The final painting, *The Nuremberg Trial*, is a six-foot oil painting of the dock viewed from above, with the fourth wall of the courtroom broken through to reveal a shattered Germany beyond the Palace of Justice. Knight's depiction of the accused in the dock, framed by the UN's guards and the defence, was strikingly realistic, setting it apart from the other artists' works, which showed the accused as caricatures. In contrast, the 'scene of destruction and devastation with flames in the background'[16] carried a more symbolic weight. As Knight had simply and modestly explained to the press, 'The subject is the dock, but I have also depicted the atmosphere of the courtroom.'[17]

The uncharacteristic symbolism in Knight's painting was likely inspired by the many scenes she witnessed in Nuremberg. In particular, the striking contrast between the orderly courtroom and the surrounding devastation must have left a powerful impression on Knight and others attending the trial – an impression vividly reflected in her diary, where she records a moment that echoes the symbolism in her painting: 'Through a window, while at breakfast I see a young German girl outlined by the devastation behind her. She is powdering her nose and draws a cupids bow in red on her lips.'[18]

In the painting one wall of the courtroom opens out to the world, serving as a realistic echo of the shelling that scarred Nuremberg's buildings. One of the buildings that Knight passed 'looked like a dolls' house with its frontage wide open… Only the third floor remained more or less whole and on it was a bed and baby in a cradle balanced dangerously near the edge, while in one corner a man and woman sat at a table eating what scraps they had been able to find…'.[19]

Despite Knight's efforts, the critical reception was mixed, possibly due to some critics growing weary of the war.[20] While some of the critics were unimpressed, the painting was a favourite of the visitors at the 1946 Royal Academy Summer Show. It remains popular today and stands as a powerful testament to a moment that continues to resonate in Europe's historical conscience.

Conclusion

One of the ethical challenges posed by the artists' representations of the trial lies in their inevitable focus on the courtroom as a space and the accused as the central subject. While the artists often caricatured the men in the dock to emphasise their much-diminished state, or their malevolence, this focus still risks glorifying the Nazi war criminals. There is a notable absence of imagery depicting the victims of the war – there are no examples in the IWM collection of sketches or paintings of the witnesses who gave testimony.

CHAPTER SEVEN

The Interpreters

Interpreters from left to right: Captain Macintosh from the British Army, translates from French into English; Margot Bortlin, translates from German into English, and Lieutenant Ernest P Uiberall.

In order for the tribunal to surmount the language barriers that divided the participants, it was necessary to create a system of rapid translation. Though there was some precedent for doing such a thing, nothing of equivalent scale had ever been attempted. Jackson, who was acutely mindful of the significance of the issue, commented 'Unless this problem is solved, the trial will be such a confusion of tongues that it will be ridiculous.'[1]

Most pre-existing systems used an approach called 'consecutive translation', which required each line to be heard, noted and then translated into the relevant language. Given there were four languages being used in the trial – English, French, Russian and German – this process would have lengthened the proceedings intolerably. As an alternative, a new method was proposed known as 'simultaneous translation'. This involved each line being translated live – or virtually live – into each language and being made available to all relevant participants at the same time.

In order for the system to be agreeable to the prosecution team, Brigadier General Robert Gill – who was Jackson's executive officer – laid out three required criteria:

1. *The mechanics had to be functional.*
2. *The court had to be informed and disciplined regarding speech.*
3. *The interpreters had to be high performing.*

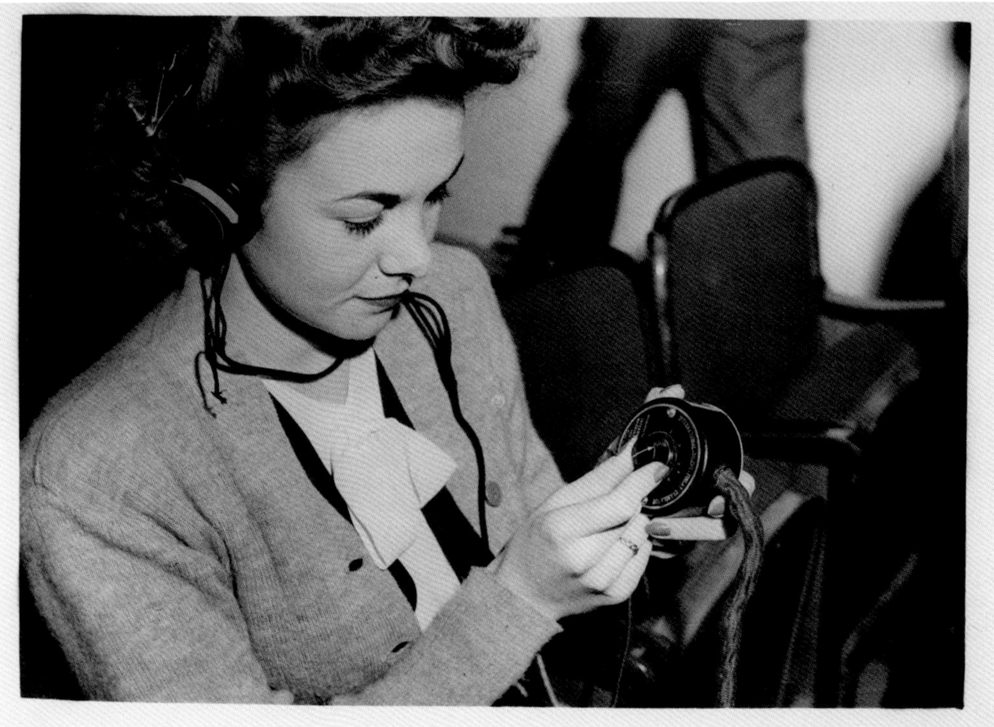

There were, therefore, both technical and personnel issues to address. The relevant hardware would have to be sourced, developed and made fit for purpose, and the right people would need to be recruited, trained and transported.

Responsibility for the hardware element fell to International Business Machines (IBM). Fortuitously, IBM had been looking at translation systems for some time and had developed the basic technology to meet the demands of Nuremberg. What they had created, however, needed first to be finessed and then shipped and installed before it could be used. This was no small undertaking given the timescales involved. And not only did the company agree to provide the system, they offered it free of charge. While at first glance an impressively altruistic gesture, in reality this was a cool-headed commercial decision. For IBM, the IMT was a remarkable and unique shop window for their new product, introducing it to a range of potential consumers in their primary target market. It was a decision that would ultimately serve them well, as the system was indeed picked up and used in other settings.

Though it was never a focus during the proceedings, or a reason for their involvement in the trial, IBM also had a wider relationship to some of the crimes under scrutiny themselves. In the late nineteenth century, the German American inventor Herman Hollerith pioneered the creation of a card-based processing system to assist the US Census Bureau. This technology was later licensed by the German businessman Willy Heidinger, who established the Deutsche Hollerith Maschinen Gesellschaft (German Hollerith Machine Corporation), or Dehomag. Hollerith then sold his American business to industrialist Charles Flint, who folded it into his new Computer-Tabulating-Recording Company (CTR). CTR would later become IBM and would make Dehomag a German subsidiary. Heidinger was a committed Nazi and supported the use of his company's technology to assist the regime's racial profiling. The data compiled and facilitated through the so-called Hollerith machine became the basis for creating the deportation lists that were used as part of the administration of mass murder. The machines were also employed by the SS to assist with the running of the concentration camps by maintaining profile cards of prisoners. Though this never became a topic of conversation during the IMT itself, in the years since it has attracted more scrutiny.

The interpretation system at Nuremberg arrived in a series of crates a few weeks before the trial started. It was fitted by specialists from IBM, who worked alongside technicians from the US Signal Corps. As it arrived so late, it wasn't possible to integrate all the cabling into the architecture of the building as it ideally would have been. For the system to function properly, everyone in the courtroom – from the judges to those in the visitor gallery – needed access to individual headphones. As a result, there were large volumes of wiring visible throughout the courtroom. Not only did this create a logistical issue, but it increased the risk of the wiring being vulnerable to accidents, which in time would create problems.

Responsibility for overseeing the recruitment and training of interpretation personnel fell to Colonel Léon Dostert.

Testing the interpreters' dial system with headphones to her head is Betty Stark, secretary to Colonel Telford Taylor of the US Executive Staff. On the dial are 5 numbers: No. 1 for the original language spoken in court; No. 2 English; No. 3 Russian; No. 4 French and No. 5 German.

Dostert was born in France in 1904, but was orphaned at a young age. During the First World War, he was befriended by some American soldiers, who eventually supported his emigration to the US in 1921. He was a very adept student of languages who followed an impressive career path, becoming Eisenhower's personal translator with an office at the Pentagon from which he worked in preparation for Nuremberg.

Though the team Dostert assembled would be translating from one language to another, all of those involved were keen to be clear that it was in fact 'interpretation' and not 'translation' that they would be doing. Translation entails engaging with written texts and having the opportunity to survey an entire manuscript before producing a version in another language. It requires time and cannot be done 'live'. Interpretation, on the other hand, involves providing an accurate account of what is being said in one language and rendering into another language almost immediately, or at least within a matter of seconds.

Dostert was looking for a highly skilled group of linguists who were fluent in the relevant languages of the trial, but could also withstand the high pressure and demands of the role. The preference was for the linguists to translate from – rather than into – their first language as this would ensure that they were as mindful of the minutiae of what was said. It was critical that every person speaking was understood as well as humanly possible, and it was felt that nuances would be better understood in their native tongue. The interpreters also needed to have clear and easily intelligible speaking voices and be able to work at speed. Dostert would later tell the *Saturday Evening Post*: 'They gave me $100,000 to recruit and set up a team of 20 interpreters as a temporary service, and be ready for a trial in three months. On the face of it, this was impossible.'[2]

All candidates were required to undergo a series of tests that would assess their ability, in terms of both their language skills and how they responded to pressure. Once a list of suitable individuals was established, the linguists then underwent a training regime to ready them for the proceedings. A version of IBM's hardware system was set up in the attic of the Palace of Justice to assist with this, allowing them to practise on the same sort of equipment they would be using during the trial

Interpreters listening to the proceedings.

through a series of role play exercises.

The team eventually comprised 36 members, who operated in 3 groups of 12. They were positioned in glass-walled booths along the side of the room, where they had a clear view of the speakers. Their positioning was important as it allowed them to use the speakers' facial expressions to inform their interpretation. Within their teams, they worked for 85 minutes at a time. While one team was working, another would be in reserve in a neighbouring room and the third would have the day off. The reserve team would have to be listening on headphones and paying attention to what was being said so that they could seamlessly take over and ensure continuity of style and vocabulary.

In addition to the interpreters who handled the main proceedings, there was a small group of auxiliary interpreters who were assigned to the judges and were responsible for dealing with any exchanges between them. There were also specialist Polish and Yiddish speakers on hand – though these weren't official languages in the trial, there were occasions when specific elements of translation from them was necessary.

To oversee the interpretation process on a day-to-day basis, a designated 'monitor' was constantly listening to the proceedings. This individual controlled a set of lights, positioned at relevant points in the courtroom, that would be illuminated if the speaker was talking faster than the interpreter was able to follow. A flashing yellow light indicated that they should slow down, and a flashing red light indicated that they should stop. The red light would be employed if something needed to be repeated, or if the interpreter had become indisposed, or was being replaced.

Everyone in the courtroom had access to the live interpretation through a personal set of headphones. The headphones had an accompanying control panel that allowed the user manually to set the language they wished to hear – channel two was English, three was Russian, four was French and five German. Channel one broadcast the live speech in whatever language it was originally delivered. Each channel was also recorded so that it could be reviewed for any discrepancies. The English translation was relayed continually to the press room through loudspeakers.

Though some of the defendants spoke excellent English, they all opted to use German in court. This gave them a little more time to consider their responses while they waited for the interpretation to occur. Translating from the defendants represented a particular challenge for the interpreters – partly because the specific grammatical structure of German, which by convention often places the verb at the end of the sentence (meaning that the overall meaning isn't fully understood until it is heard in its entirety), and partly because of their euphemistic use of language. The Nazis devised and employed a parallel vocabulary to occlude the truth of what was actually being referred to, and the interpreters in court had to navigate this as they went about their jobs. Over time the court became more adept at understanding these references, and the euphemisms were exposed for what they were.

There was universal agreement that the translation system,

Nuremberg Dock by Joseph Otto Flatter. Twenty of the defendants in the Nuremberg trial are portrayed in the courtroom with a row of US military policemen in the background. Many of the defendants are listening to the proceedings with headphones.

both in terms of hardware and personnel, was critical to the IMT, but it was not completely infallible – and when it didn't work the proceedings ground to a halt. On one occasion, it suddenly malfunctioned entirely, forcing the trial to be suspended while the issue was investigated. An engineer traced the main cable from the control panel and, eventually, found that a section that ran under the carpet of two steps, which led down into the well of the court, had been worn through by weeks of footfall. The break was repaired and the trial was able to continue.

CHAPTER EIGHT

The Proceedings

ver the course of 315 days, the Nuremberg trial unfolded in structured phases. The prosecution opened the case, presenting its arguments over 73 days until 4 March 1946. The defence followed shortly after, beginning on 8 March and concluding on 31 August. The judges then withdrew to deliberate over the verdicts for a month, considering the evidence, before delivering their verdicts on 1 October.

Lord Justice Lawrence, Nuremberg, 1946 by Laura Knight.

Determined to avoid any accusations of bias, the Allies took care to design the IMT with fairness in mind. Its procedures blended elements from the legal systems of the participating nations, including aspects of Germany's own. Notably, defence counsels were granted access to the prosecution's evidence – a rule unfamiliar to the American lawyers present. Court interpreter Peter Uiberall recalled their discomfort and unfamiliarity with this system:

> And I remember how they were complaining in the beginning, '...how can I bring something in that is a surprise and therefore will get the defendant to make an admission, if I have to tell his defence counsel before...?'[1]

Uiberall, an Austrian Jewish refugee, was impressed with the presiding judge, Lord Justice Lawrence, who was pivotal in maintaining the principle of fairness at Nuremberg. Widely respected by both Allied and German lawyers, Uiberall described him as a 'fabulous'[2] judge, whose impartiality and even-handedness earned him universal admiration. He kept the courtroom in check, often challenging overlong arguments with the pointed question: 'Is all this detail real[ly] necessary?'[3]

One particularly memorable moment for Uiberall came during a confrontation with Göring. After attempting to slap a witness for swearing at him as he left court, Göring was reprimanded by Lawrence, and it was Uiberall's duty to interpret for the judge:

> ...as the court room had emptied completely...the presiding judge gave Göring a lecture about behaviour and told him if this would happen once again, he would be confined to bread and water etc. and he would be deprived of his exercise rights etc. And I found myself in the enviable position of being able to deliver the lecture in German to Hermann Göring – Fat Hermann – he was a strange impression this man, in this much too large uniform, he didn't look like anything, let alone like the feared Göring who was responsible for so many terrible crimes.[4]

Despite such moments, Göring and the other defendants held Lawrence in high regard. As well as presiding over the proceedings in an 'impeccably just'[5] way, his popularity was also attributed to his personal charm and good manners. Neave gathered evidence for the War Crimes Executive, then worked at the trial. Neave recalls his daily arrival at the Palace of Justice – dressed in a black coat and striped trousers – as 'one of the sights of ruined Nuremberg'.[6] As he entered the court, he would pause to bow formally to all counsel before taking his seat.

Captain Barous (seated) and M Prochta inspecting the Czechoslovak 'Black Book'. Compiled by the Czech Ministry of the Interior, this was made up of documentary and photographic evidence showing atrocities committed by the Nazis during the occupation.

Clerks binding reams of evidence collated for presentation at the trial.

The Evidence

Rudolf Hess having a meal during his trial at Nuremberg.

The trial placed a strong emphasis on documentary evidence, and the Allies had recovered a vast archive of Nazi records. While this approach provided a credible foundation for the trial, it also contributed to the slow pace of the proceedings. The sheer volume of material presented caused the proceedings to drag, but the requirement for simultaneously translation into four languages compounded the delays further, particularly during the prosecution. Reuters' correspondent, Maynes, found the 'first few months absolutely boring'[7] as the defendants were largely silent, barred from interjecting. Roberts, who cross-examined Jodl, echoed this sentiment.

The pace of the trial was not helped by the prosecutors themselves, who at times struggled to manage the documentation skilfully. The same document was often submitted twice as the lawyers became overwhelmed occasionally by the paper evidence. Lawrence, mindful of these frustrating disruptions, would intervene to push things along. On 5 February 1946, he urged French prosecutor M Faure to 'cut down his spate of documents and press on with the evidence',[8] after the French had already presented more than 1,200 documents to the court.

Though many observers and journalists found the heavy reliance on documents tedious, some of the trial's legal minds recognised their power. Among them was US prosecutor Benjamin Ferencz, who at the first of the subsequent American trials that followed the IMT convicted members of the *Einsatzgruppen* for mass murder in the German-occupied East. He relied on SS reports detailing the number of killings in the Soviet Union. For him, such records were more incriminating than any witness. 'Witness testimony is the worst evidence', he stated bluntly.[9]

The Defining Moments

Amid the procedural grind of the trial, certain moments stood out. The screening of footage from the liberation of concentration camps was one of these instances, as was the cross-examination of Göring, who remained bullish and

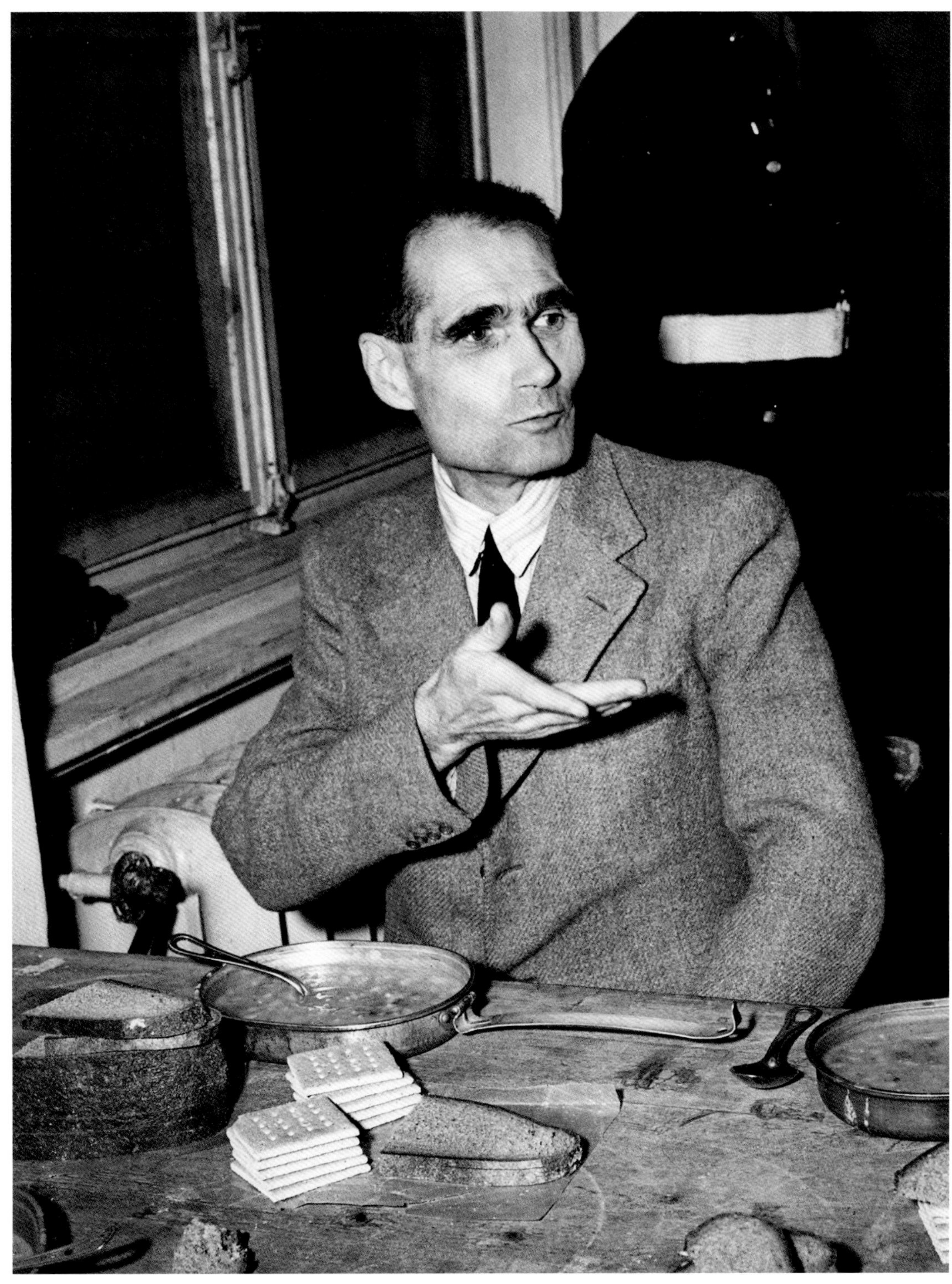

truculent throughout. But equally memorable – though often absent from the official transcript – were the many episodes of humour that punctuated the proceedings. Humour helped to relieve the tedium of the trial and offered an escape from the grim subject matter. It was also a weapon used by both the prosecution and the defendants to ridicule their opponents. Judge Lawrence frequently had to reprimand the court for laughing, while the press eagerly recorded these lighter moments.

A recurring source of amusement was Lawrence's impatience, particularly during Colonel Robert Storey's presentation against the Reich Cabinet. When Storey showed photos of Hitler, Göring and other leading Nazis in *Sturmabteilung* (SA)uniform, Lawrence dryly asked, 'Is there any doubt then that Hitler and Göring were members of the S.A.?'[10] Storey's embarrassment proved highly entertaining to the defendants, who smirked, grinned and 'finally laugh[ed] outright'.[11]

The most consistent source of humour was Hess. Claiming amnesia from the outset, he baffled US military psychiatrists before suddenly announcing on 29 November that his memory had returned. Hess's blurted out plea of '*Nein*' – followed by Lawrence's deadpan response, 'That will be entered as a plea of not guilty'[12] – was another moment of hilarity for the court. Perhaps because the defendants failed to grasp the seriousness of the trial, or were so accustomed to power that they had lost all sense of shame, their behaviour could be startlingly uninhibited.

Screenings and Witnesses

As powerful as the German documents were, they could not fully convey the lived experience of Nazi brutality. Statistics on forced labourers, murder and detailed reports on the concentration camps, even when delivered by a powerful orator such as Justice Jackson, lacked the emotional weight and immediacy of first-hand testimony. As US Prosecutor Major Walsh conceded, when presenting the case for the persecution of the Jews, 'The slaughter of the Jews of Europe cannot be expressed in figures alone...yet these cold, stark, brutal facts and figures, largely drawn from the defendant's own sources and submitted in evidence before the tribunal defy rebuttal.'[13]

The recognition of the limits of documentary evidence led to a shift in strategy. More live witnesses were called and the screening of the first film, originally scheduled for the concentration camp case, was brought forward during the case on the *Anschluss* of Austria, just eight days into the trial.

The film, *Nazi Concentration Camps*, was an hour-long compilation of footage from 12 camps uncovered by American and British troops as they advanced into Germany and Austria. It drew on the cameramen's caption sheets, with the film shown in mute but accompanied by live commentary read in court. The film was produced by John Ford and directed by Ray Kellogg, a special effects expert who worked in Hollywood.

In keeping with the evidentiary procedure, the film begins and ends with affidavits from the filmmakers, read aloud as they appeared on screen. A map marked the locations of 300 camps across Europe, before showing scenes of devastation, beginning with Tekla camp and ending with the liberation of Bergen-Belsen. The final scenes of SS guards forced to bury the dead, and a bulldozer pushing naked corpses into mass graves, left an unshakeable impression on all who witnessed them.

Although some of the footage had previously appeared in newsreels, much of it was new to the courtroom. The film's unflinching coverage of Nazi brutality led to it being dubbed the 'horror film'.[14] One report listed its contents starkly:

> Crematoriums, heaped corpses of unknown victims, brutal guards and dogs, gas chambers, instruments of torture, mass graves, emaciated and starving slaves, laboratories for human guinea-pig experiments, electrified-wiring – these and countless other nightmares flickered on the screens.[15]

The screening left a profound impact. One reporter noted that when the lights came up, the courtroom remained silent for two minutes.[16] The *Daily Herald* reported that the defence counsel, who had already seen the film before, 'emerged from their second ordeal ashen-faced and shaken'.[17]

Press coverage focused heavily on the reactions of the defendants, which many found more interesting than the film itself. This was no accident. The organisers had installed fluorescent lighting in the dock to ensure the defendants' reactions were visible during the screenings, and stationed the official psychiatrists, Kelley and Gilbert, at either end to observe their responses closely.

Though a handful of the defendants seemed unmoved, or feigned indifference, most were visibly affected by the screening of *Nazi Concentration Camps*. Vassiltchikov, an interpreter, observed the accused during the screening and recalled that many wore glasses, partly to shield themselves from the lights, but also to 'hide their emotions'.[18] Calvocoressi was sceptical of the film's evidentiary value, but acknowledged its psychological impact:

> ...to have refused to believe that certain things have happened... when the film was put on... they were, like everybody else... shaken, but they were shaken more by the enormity of it... That there had been such things as concentration camps and labour camps, and that these had been pretty unpleasant places, must have been reasonably well known to everybody. But that is one thing and actually seeing on a film, a huge number of corpses and even more so of people who are not quite corpses yet...[19]

For Neave the film offered an opportunity to gauge the guilt of the accused:

> As the lights went up, I looked at the dock. The defendants remained seated, as if turned to stone. They were slow to rise when the judges filed out in disgusted silence. During the showing of the film, the dock, as a measure of security was picked out by small spotlights. Few of the defendants could bear to watch the whole film. Schacht, who had personal experience of a concentration camp, sat with his back to the screen.
>
> I cannot forget the sudden vision of those twisted guilty faces, some, like Funk and Fritzsche, with tears on their cheeks. I sometimes dream of it. I sought for any signs of true remorse and did not find them. These were crocodile tears. They wept for themselves, not for the dead. They

Defendants in the dock during the trial. Left to right: Göring, Hess, von Ribbentrop, Keitel, Kaltenbrunner, Rosenberg, Frank, Frick, Streicher, Funk, Schacht, Dönitz, Raeder, von Schirach, Sauckel, Jodl, von Papen, Seyss-Inquart, Speer, von Neurath and Fritzsche.

feared for their own necks as they watched films of humble men and women executed by the S.S.[20]

Neave's cynicism towards the apparent remorse of the defendants was valid. It's difficult to credit this group of hardened Nazis with the capacity for genuine self-reflection. Yet his observation – that the film forced them to confront the reality that their crimes had caught up with them – rings true. It also highlights the tactical value of *Nazi Concentration Camps* in weakening the resolve of the accused, who were visibly shaken by the experience.

The screening also overshadowed other films that were

shown during the trial. *The Nazi Plan*, shown on 11 December 1945, was a four-hour compilation of captured German footage, intended to reinforce the conspiracy charges in counts one and two of the indictment. Yet its impact was mixed. As a visual chronicle of the rise of the Nazi party, it included scenes of rallies and German military conquests that stirred nostalgia in the defendants. Filled with excitement, the accused practically re-enacted the Nazi parades on the screen, to the bemusement of the court:

As the first woman witness at the Nuremberg trial, Madame Marie Claude Vaillant-Couturier gave a graphic and horrifying account of her two and a half years in Nazi concentration camps.

> Göring nudged Hess heartily...Rudolf stared fascinated at the earlier Rudolf...Göring bounced with excitement... Baldur von Schirach trembled with excitement when film showed him presenting German youth to the Fuhrer.[21]

Even the English interpreter, unaware that his microphone was still live during the screening, remarked that 'Göring is getting a big kick out of this.'[22] But journalist Bernard Murphy also noticed how the film undermined the Nazis' constructed propaganda image. 'In the darkness,' he wrote, 'the Court lost all its judicial atmosphere. The American soldiers could not refrain from hearty laughter as Hitler pranced and ranted in pantomime.'[23]

Fortunately for the prosecution, the concluding reel of *The Nazi Plan* had a more sobering effect. Subtitled *Wars of Aggression, 1939 to 1944*, Commander Donovan introduced the screening with the words: 'In September 1939 the Nazis launched the first of a series of catastrophic wars, terminated only by the military collapse of Germany...'.[24] The reel concluded with footage following the 20 July 1944 bomb plot to assassinate Hitler, including 5 minutes from the 11-hour Nazi propaganda epic, the *People's Court Trial Concerning Plot of 20 July Judge Freisler Presiding*. Though a longer version was intended for later use in the Hans Frank case, even this brief glimpse of Nazi justice had the desired effect on the accused, as Göring confided to a US psychiatrist:

> You know what hurt me more than even the concentration camp film, bad as it was? It was that loudmouth, Freisler. It actually made me squirm, the way he screamed at the defendants. After all, these were generals, not yet proven

guilty. I tell you, I could have died of shame.[25]

Witnesses

While the film screenings left a powerful visual impression, it was the testimony of survivors that gave voice to the human cost behind the devastating footage. The account given by Madame Marie Claude Vaillant-Couturier, a survivor of Auschwitz and Ravensbrück, stood out for its emotional weight. Called to the stand on 28 January 1946 by the French prosecution, she was the first female witness to testify at the IMT. A communist deputy and widow of the editor of *L'Humanité*, Vaillant-Couturier had been arrested by the Vichy police, handed over to the Germans and transported to Auschwitz with 230 other French women. Of them: only 49 survived. Speaking 'in a firm dispassionate voice',[26] she described the brutal experiences of women at Auschwitz: selections, gassing, the camp orchestra, ordered to play while selections for new arrivals took place, and sterilisations, alongside other horrors. Her account gave names and faces to her murdered friends and comrades, as well the anonymous victims seen in the films. Her veracious testimony also withstood cross-examination, particularly her claim that by 1944 knowledge of the camps was spreading beyond their fences, as guards and *Kapos* were reassigned to combat duties and factory work.

Her testimony was even more credible due to her strong and dignified bearing, which left a strong impression on the court. She stared down the defendants, who were transfixed by her presence: 'All the accused in the dock kept their eyes fixed on Madame Couturier,' one observer noted. 'Some of them at times hung their heads.'[27] Hess followed every word, while Göring appeared 'pale and downcast' and 'von Papen covered his face with his hands'.[28] Like others who testified, Vaillant-Couturier took the opportunity to confront her former oppressors:

> Before she left the courtroom she walked slowly right across the front of the dock, staring into the faces of the accused men. Then, as she passed through the doorway, she turned and directed a last bitter stare at them.[29]

Hermann Göring, wearing headphones and reading a document, sits in the courtroom witness box. He is flanked by two American military policemen.

The Cross-Examination of Göring

The examination and cross-examination of Göring was one of the defining episodes of the trial. As the highest-ranking Nazi in the dock, Göring was also its dominant character. His influence was so pronounced that, even before the trial, there were fears he would undermine the prosecution's case and even the legitimacy of the trial. These concerns proved well-founded. Göring's testimony, which began on 13 March and lasted almost five days, was a powerful, orchestrated defence. Justice Lawrence, usually praised for his fairness, indulged Göring, enabling him to deliver an extended speech. He described the rise of the Nazi party as a justified response to the humiliation of 1918, omitting key events like the Reichstag fire and justifying the anti-democratic measures, including concentration camps, as necessary for national stability. It was an impressive performance, met with applause and back-slapping from his fellow defendants, and even admiration from the press.

Jackson began his cross-examination of Göring on 18 March, continuing for almost five sessions. But the prosecution, which had lost control of the courtroom, struggled to regain its footing. Jackson lacked the courtroom experience to challenge Göring's skilful rhetoric. As Uiberall tactfully recalled, Jackson once posed a legal question, prompting Göring to reply: 'I can't answer that question

because *I* was not the leading jurist in my country, thank God!'[30] It was a direct slight, aimed at Jackson, and one that exposed the mismatched dynamics.

Göring's strategy was simple: frustrate the prosecution. He challenged the documents on technicalities, denied his involvement in key events and exploited the complicated nature of the Nazi regime's bureaucracy to cast doubt on almost any evidence. He repeatedly ignored procedural rules, offering long-winded justifications instead of simple yes and no answers, and used every opportunity to inject propaganda into his responses and goad the prosecution. Jackson, increasingly infuriated, eventually appealed to Lawrence, accusing him of giving Göring too much freedom and allowing the trial to drift off course. It was an admission of defeat and a misstep which alienated Jackson from his colleagues on the bench. Calvocoressi noted how it marked a low point in the trial, and a moment when the prosecution needed quickly to regain control.

Fortunately for the prosecution, when Jackson handed over to Maxwell Fyfe, the case passed into the hands of a seasoned courtroom lawyer. He was so effective that he proved a draw for the court staff:

> As I mentioned, my colleagues and I, if we were not on duty in the courtroom and we knew that Sir David Maxwell-Fyfe was going to be *on,* as we called it, we made sure that we were present to listen. He was very, very, effective and very good, very strong.[31]

Taking over the cross-examination on 20 March, Maxwell Fyfe avoided the political arguments that played into Göring's strategy and instead focused on the Luftwaffe chief's criminal acts – most notably, the execution of 49 RAF POW who had escaped from Stalag Luft III, one of the 6 Luftwaffe-run POW camps under Göring's command. Göring claimed ignorance, insisting he had been on holiday and had not been informed until days after. As Hitler was known to take the issue of escaping Allied airmen very seriously, the claim was implausible. With sly charm and the precision of an experienced criminal lawyer, Maxwell Fyfe demolished

Hermann Göring, commanding and often combative, used the trials as a stage to defend the Nazi regime.

Göring's defence in under two sessions. As Neave admiringly recalled, 'Maxwell-Fyfe skilfully tested his alibi as if he were prosecuting a burglar at the old bailey.'[32]

He then turned to Göring's knowledge of the treatment of Jews and forced labourers. Göring denied that he, or Hitler, knew about the extermination policy, the camps or the scale of Nazi atrocities – claims that Maxwell Fyfe proved absurd. By the time Maxwell Fyfe had handed over to the Soviet prosecutor General Rudenko, Göring had weakened. Rudenko, continuing the same line of questioning, provoked an even more dramatic reaction. Göring ended the session ranting his denials:

> **Rudenko**: 'You must have been aware of the death of millions of innocent people?'
> **Göring** (Grabbing the side of the witness box) 'No I did not know about them or cause them.'
> **Rudenko**: 'You had to know about these facts.'
> **Göring**: 'Why did I have to know? Either I knew them or I didn't know them. You can only say that I was negligent in not finding them out.'
> **Rudenko**: 'You ought to know better. Millions of Germans know about them and you didn't?'
> **Göring**: (shouting) 'Millions of Germans did not know about them. That is not an established fact.'[33]

Years later Maxwell Fyfe admitted that he was not entirely immune to Göring's charm, but that he had a simple strategy: avoid eye contact to prevent being drawn in and making him laugh. Unlike Jackson, who would quickly abandon lines of questioning when Göring pushed back, Maxwell Fyfe was cunning and persistent. Much of Jackson's documentary evidence was damning, but he failed to push his points home. However, Jackson's approach, engaging Göring on the high politics of the Nazi regime, was understandable. As chief prosecutor and a legal expert, it may have seemed natural to confront Göring's narrative directly. But vanity may have also played a part. Jackson appeared to seek not just a legal victory, but also a personal one: an admission of guilt from the regime's most prominent surviving figure. Göring, however,

The Rt Hon Sir David Maxwell Fyfe, KC, Nuremberg, 1946 by Laura Knight.

was never going to give him that.

Maxwell Fyfe, on the other hand, recognised that a confession wasn't needed. His goal, instead, was to expose the implausibility of Göring's defences. His dogged and methodical questioning made Göring's defence appear ridiculous and hollow. In just over a day he dismantled Göring's authority and restored the prosecution's credibility, rescuing it from the setback suffered under Jackson's cross-examination.

The Verdicts and Sentencing

Out of the 22 defendants (including Bormann who was tried in absentia), 3 were acquitted, 12 were sentenced to death and the rest served prison sentences. Speer and six others escaped execution. The Tribunal chose hanging as the method of execution, rejecting alternatives such as the guillotine or firing squad. This decision provoked outrage from the convicted military leaders, who believed that they deserved to be shot in recognition of their status as officers. Jodl and Keitel were shocked and uttered almost the same words, 'Death – by hanging! –That, at least, I did not deserve.'[34] Keitel and Göring appealed to the Allied Control Council for their method of execution to be changed to shooting, but their requests were denied.

The symbolism of hanging was deliberate – a final disgrace to the German officer class, who had expected honourable treatment. It also shocked many ordinary Germans. Elfriede Lawrence, a young woman from Nuremberg working at the IMT as a clerk, remembered how upset her stepfather was by the decision. He considered Jodl and Keitel as soldiers

fulfilling their duty and believed the *Wehrmacht* to be an organisation innocent of war crimes.

Laura Knight's *Sketch for 'The Nuremberg Trial'* depicting a section of the defendants' box. From left to right: Göring, Hess, von Ribbentrop and Keitel. An American guard stands behind them.

The Executions and Göring's Suicide

The executions took place in the early hours on 16 October 1946, between 1.14am and 2.15am, on two specially constructed gallows in the prison gymnasium of the Palace of Justice. The executions were not photographed or filmed, but two newspaper correspondents from each of the occupying powers were present to cover this final act. The rest of the press waited nearby, receiving a list of the condemned, along with the order and time of execution. Official photographs of the bodies were taken after death for record purposes and the remains were inspected by the Allied commissioners and two German representatives.

Originally the Allied Control Council had ruled that the executions would be held in private, 'without publicity'.[35] But, following pressure from the press, the decision was reconsidered. A ballot was held to determine which journalists could attend. Hugh Baillie, head of the United Press of America, argued that the 'people' had 'a very definite interest' in the final fate of the condemned Nazis, especially the friends and family of Americans who had died fighting the regime.[36] American officials also feared that secrecy might fuel rumours that some of the Nazi leaders were still alive.[37] In total, around 30 witnesses were present, including Wilhelm Hoegner, the Bavarian President of Justice, reappointed after having been dismissed by Hans Frank in the Nazi era. A court stenographer was also present to record the condemned men's final words.

Göring was scheduled to hang first, but at 10.45pm on 15 October – just hours before his execution – he took his own life by swallowing cyanide. In his suicide note, he explained that, at the time of his capture, he had three pills hidden: one in the clothes he was wearing, which was found by guards, another concealed in cream within his toiletry bag and one secreted somewhere on his body. According to Maynes, American guards believed Göring had resolved to commit suicide after learning that his appeal to be shot had

been denied. Others speculated that his objection to hanging stemmed more from fear than honour. Göring confided in Kelley that he was in dread of the method, having seen the photos of Benito Mussolini and his mistress being publicly hung in Rome.[38] His true motivation remains uncertain. In the suicide note and letters he left in his cell, Göring states that the dishonour of being hanged by his enemies was the deciding factor. The act was also consistent with his conduct throughout the proceedings – defiant and undermining the legitimacy of the trial whenever possible. His suicide was met with mixed reactions. In Berlin some Nazi sympathisers expressed their admiration. 'At least he did not give them the satisfaction of seeing him hang,' said Max Speet,[39] a former German Army captain. Another remarked that 'Old Hermann foxed 'em'.[40]

Despite Göring's suicide, the executions went ahead as planned, with von Ribbentrop executed first, followed by Keitel. According to Maynes, who spoke with eyewitnesses who attended the executions, they were a 'botched job'. [41] This was substantiated by the American correspondent Gault MacGowan of the *New York Sun*, who reported that 'an official medical inspection below the platform revealed a shambles'.[42] Keitel was dangling for 23 minutes before he died, and the American executioner, Master Sergeant John C Woods, had to go down under the scaffold and tug on the legs of one of the men to ensure he was dead. Woods later claimed he had not been given the prisoners' body weights to calculate proper drop lengths; others blamed his inexperience and argued that the task should have gone to British hangman Albert Pierrepoint.[43]

The announcement of the executions was also bungled. Due to the pre-circulation of the execution list, the timing of Göring's suicide, and the press corps being held in the jail until the hangings were complete, the German-based American news agency DANA prematurely released the story at 2.00am, incorrectly stating that 11, including Göring, had been executed. This error was picked up internationally, with some British newspapers' 'STOP PRESS' sections repeating the mistake.

The executed men were cremated in secret at a Munich crematorium and their ashes scattered in the River Isar to prevent any site of pilgrimage. On 23 October, 11 photographs of the bodies – including Göring's – were distributed to the American, Soviet and French press, but were withheld from the British press. Prime Minister Clement Attlee appealed to British editors not to publish the images.

Hjalmar Schacht at a press interview half an hour after he was released.

The Verdicts

Four charges were brought against the Nazis:

Count one: the common plan or conspiracy
Count two: crimes against peace
Count three: war crimes
Count four: crimes against humanity

Hermann Göring:
Guilty on all four counts; sentenced to death by hanging (committed suicide before execution).

Rudolf Hess:
Guilty on counts of conspiracy and crimes against the peace; sentenced to life in prison.

Joachim von Ribbentrop:
Guilty on all four counts; sentenced to death by hanging.

Wilhelm Keitel:
Guilty on all four counts; sentenced to death by hanging.

Ernst Kaltenbrunner:
Guilty of war crimes and crimes against humanity; sentenced to death by hanging.

Alfred Rosenberg:
Guilty on all four counts; sentenced to death by hanging.

Hans Frank:
Guilty of war crimes and crimes against humanity; sentenced to death by hanging.

Wilhelm Frick:
Guilty of crimes against the peace, war crimes and crimes against humanity; sentenced to death by hanging.

Julius Streicher:
Guilty of crimes against humanity; sentenced to death by hanging.

Walther Funk:
Guilty of crimes against the peace, war crimes and crimes against humanity; sentenced to life in prison.

Hjalmar Schacht:
Acquitted.

Karl Dönitz:
Guilty of crimes against the peace and war crimes; sentenced to ten years in prison.

Erich Raeder:
Guilty of conspiracy, crimes against the peace and war crimes; sentenced to life in prison.

Baldur von Schirach:
Guilty of crimes against humanity; sentenced to 20 years in prison.

Fritz Sauckel:
Guilty of war crimes and crimes against humanity; sentenced to death by hanging.

Alfred Jodl:
Guilty on all four counts; sentenced to death by hanging.

Martin Bormann:
Guilty of war crimes and crimes against humanity; sentenced to death by hanging.

Franz von Papen:
Acquitted.

Arthur Seyss-Inquart:
Guilty of crimes against the peace, war crimes and crimes against humanity; sentenced to death by hanging.

Albert Speer:
Guilty of war crimes and crimes against humanity; sentenced to 20 years in prison.

Konstantin Freiherr von Neurath:
Guilty on all four counts; sentenced to 15 years in prison.

Hans Fritzsche:
Acquitted.

The Allied Control Council refused to give clemency to the Nazis found guilty and the sentences were put into full effect.

CHAPTER NINE

The Legacy of Nuremberg

Hersch Lauterpacht on the day he 'took silk' (became King's Counsel) in 1949. He is pictured with Reynold Bennett (a distant relative), Rachel (his wife) and Inka Katz (his only close relative to survive the Holocaust).

The legacy of the Nuremberg trial extended long after its verdicts were announced and has become an integral part of the collective memory of the Second World War. The proceedings continue to attract the attention of filmmakers and commentators to this day. For many the trial marked a turning point, not only in how justice was pursued on an international scale, but also in how the world confronted the moral weight of the Nazi regime's crimes. However, reactions to the trial at the time were far from unanimous. Reuters' correspondent, Seaghan Maynes, for instance, thought it was a revenge trial, and the legal process suspect. For survivors of the Nazi regime, the trial evoked complex responses. Michael Etkind, a Polish Jew from Łódź, who survived Buchenwald and Sonnenberg concentration camps, viewed the trial with a sense of detachment. His disinterest stemmed not from doubt of their legality, but because they were not justice, rather a futile gesture. In his view, the prosecution of a 'few dozen' men could not account for the 'Germans and Austrians, there were millions of them, who were murderers, [and those] who took part in the murders [of] not thousands, but millions'.[1] Etkind was also disheartened by the discourse surrounding the trial, particularly correspondence published in the *Picture Post*, where readers expressed the desire for forgiveness of the accused men on Christian grounds. One letter, from a teacher, resonated with Etkind's own thoughts: 'What right have we to forgive, only the dead and God have the right to forgive.'[2]

The Documents

While the trial's pace was slow and its atmosphere subdued – its drama buried beneath piles of dry, official documents – the documentary evidence presented had the power to leave a lasting impression on those who engaged with them closely. For court administrator Elfriede Lawrence, who was responsible for typing documents as they were translated, it was only through this process that she gained a profound and unsettling understanding of the true nature of the regime she had lived under. She typed the translation of documents from the Wannsee Conference, including papers on the Final Solution – the Nazi plan to murder the Jews of Europe – as well as harrowing accounts from concentration camp survivors. When she recounted these to her neighbours, fellow ordinary Germans, their reaction was one of denial, claiming 'Germans just don't behave like that'.[3]

There will always be those who deny or downplay the crimes of the Nazi regime, but the sheer volume of evidence amassed and presented at Nuremberg leaves little room for doubt. Even some of the trial's early critics, who believed giving the perpetrators a legal platform was unnecessary or even dangerous, were ultimately swayed by the trial's success. Lord Vansittart, who had initially opposed the idea of a war crimes trial, was persuaded by the rigorous nature of its investigations:

> I am bound to say, however, that the magnitude and thoroughness of the revelations thus far brought forth at Nuremberg make its proceedings a valuable historic record. I hope they will convince the world, including some Germans, what we were really up against.[4]

Legacy in Film

The legacy of the trial is also preserved in the films produced during the proceedings, including both the official courtroom proceedings and the evidence films that were submitted by the prosecution. Today the surviving footage gives us a rare sense of the court's atmosphere, capturing moments of drama and interaction that the written transcripts cannot convey.

These films formed the basis of two official documentaries on the IMT. The first, a 1946 Soviet production, *The Nuremberg Trial – A film document of the trial of the principal German war criminals* (also known as *The Judgment of the Nations*), followed by the American film *Nuremberg: Its Lesson for Today* (1948). Both films succeeded in condensing the lengthy proceedings into accessible narratives, drawing effectively on the evidence of films and broader Allied wartime footage to enhance their impact. But there was also a marked absence of witness testimony, featuring only five witnesses in the American film and none in the Soviet film.

Produced in the immediate aftermath of the war, both films were hampered by the political climate of the time. Roman Karmen's Soviet film, for instance, offered a diluted account of the Holocaust and reflected the cooling Soviet attitude towards the Allies. The resulting Soviet bias – particularly the omission of Allied contributions to Germany's defeat – diminished the film's credibility in the West. Meanwhile the American production, directed by Stuart Schulberg, faced delays due to wrangles over its focus and shifting political attitudes on post-war Germany. There were concerns over the film's potentially negative impact on German morale. These anxieties postponed the film's release by seven months and prevented the production of a planned American domestic version.

The Use of Film in War Crimes Trials

The use of film at Nuremberg set a precedent that would shape the conduct of later war crimes trials. At the trial of Adolf Eichmann in 1961, the courtroom was fully equipped for television broadcast, allowing the proceedings to be transmitted internationally. On 8 June that year, 90 minutes of evidentiary film – much of it previously shown at Nuremberg – was screened in the courtroom. As at the IMT, the organisers were keen for the public to witness the reactions of the accused to the films of Nazi atrocities and the concentration camps. A camera was trained on the witness box, capturing Eichmann's expression as he watched the footage. The resulting broadcast coverage of session 70 alternated between Eichmann's impassive reaction and the harrowing footage on screen. The trial of Klaus Barbie marked the first time a French court permitted televised coverage. The footage was edited down to 37 daily episodes, each running for 2 hours. These examples illustrate how television enabled a more expansive and accessible form of courtroom documentation, overcoming the logistical and financial limitations of previous cinematic methods. The televisual format also introduced a new dynamic: by shaping the trials into serialised narratives, it risked reducing the gravity of the proceedings into a 'soap opera'.[5]

The practices established at Nuremberg found a more direct continuation in the work of the International Criminal Tribunal for Yugoslava (ICTY) and International Criminal Tribunal for Rwanda (ICTR), where video became an integral part in the prosecution of war crimes, genocide and crimes against humanity. In the course of their investigations in Yugoslavia and Rwanda, the UN International Tribunals gathered over 11,000 hours of analogue and digital video evidence, spanning more than 20 different formats. The proceedings themselves were also comprehensively recorded; the ICTY alone amassed 60,000 hours of video coverage. The importance of this video record as part of the tribunal's legacy is acknowledged on the website for the United Nations International Residual Mechanism for Criminal Tribunals, where it is stated that:

> The Prosecution's Evidence Collection is a unique repository of material telling the story of the crimes committed in the Balkans and Rwanda, the people who allegedly planned and perpetrated those crimes, and their victims.
>
> Most importantly, the Collection is still at the core of much of the Prosecution's work and national jurisdictions' accountability efforts.[6]

Witnesses on Screen

The most famous film on the Nuremberg trials is the Hollywood feature *Judgment at Nuremberg* (1961), though it does not depict the IMT itself. Instead, it dramatises the so-called 'Judges' Trial', one of the subsequent Nuremberg trials. Despite this, the film has come to symbolise the Nuremberg trials. This may have been a deliberate choice by director Stanley Kramer, whose film blends themes, moments and personalities from this trial and the IMT. For instance, the screening of the concentration camp footage – a key event at the IMT – is introduced into the re-creation of the judges' trial. The script also includes quotes that appear to echo the IMT proceedings or refer to actions around it, such as the moment when Marlene Dietrich's character speaks of her husband's shame, as a German general, facing hanging rather than the firing squad, likely alluding to Jodl's protest at the manner of his death. The film's powerful fictional witnesses, who spoke at the stand in *Judgment at Nuremberg*, may have also influenced later documentary filmmakers, encouraging a shift towards the testimonies of real individuals. Marcel Ophüls's four-hour film *The Memory of Justice* (1976) exemplifies this approach. Drawing on 50 hours of the original trial footage, Ophüls supplemented archival material with new interviews, including conversations with members of the prosecution team and with the former defendants, such as Dönitz and Speer, effectively re-examining their roles in the Nazi regime. More recent documentaries, such as Christian Delage's *Nuremberg: The Nazis Facing their Crimes* (2006) and Lutz Becker's *Nuremberg in History* (2006), have also shifted the focus from wartime footage towards interviews with the trial participants and original witness testimonies, such as Marie Claude Vaillant-Couturier. This change in emphasis reflects a desire to restage the trial as a means to develop a deeper moral inquiry and retrospectively to give greater voice to the victims, whose presence was often missing in the original proceedings.

Legacies

This scribbled note, written around 1944, reveals Raphael Lemkin's thinking around the word 'genocide'.

Nuremberg changed international justice, but this impact wasn't necessarily felt immediately. Indeed, it would be over 50 years until the baton raised by the legal professionals at the IMT was grasped by a future generation. Two of the lawyers, whose work had the most significant role in the trial's legacy, were not among the frontline prosecution team. They were Hersch Lauterpacht and Raphael Lemkin. Both had been bought up and educated in Lviv and both had fled before the Nazis' arrival. Both had also lost family in the Holocaust.

Lemkin had developed a concept for an international crime that referred to the attempt to destroy a group, in whole or in part. He first struck upon the idea while trying to find a legal means of responding to the mass murder of the Armenians by the Ottoman Turks during the First World War. The term that Lemkin conceived for the crime he was trying to define was genocide. He invented it by combining the words *genos*, from the Greek for 'race' or 'family', and *cide*, from the Latin for 'kill'. 'Genocide' did not feature as a discrete offence at Nuremberg, but appeared within the language of the charges.

Lauterpacht had advocated for the creation of an alternative legal concept that was aimed at the inalienable rights of the individual. He referred to this as 'crimes against humanity'. For Lauterpacht, it was critical that civilians were protected by international law as a fundamental principle. As laid out in the London Charter, crimes against humanity could be defined as 'murder, extermination, enslavement, deportation, and other inhumane acts committed against civilian populations, before or during the war; or persecutions on political, racial or religious grounds in execution of or in connection with any crime within the jurisdiction of the Tribunal, whether or not in violation of the domestic law of the country where perpetrated'.[7]

Genocide was enshrined into international law in 1948 in the Convention on the Prevention and Punishment of the Crime of Genocide (also known as the Genocide Convention). It was a significant moment, but it would not be until the latter part of the century that the law was actually used as part of a criminal case. The peace that followed the end of the

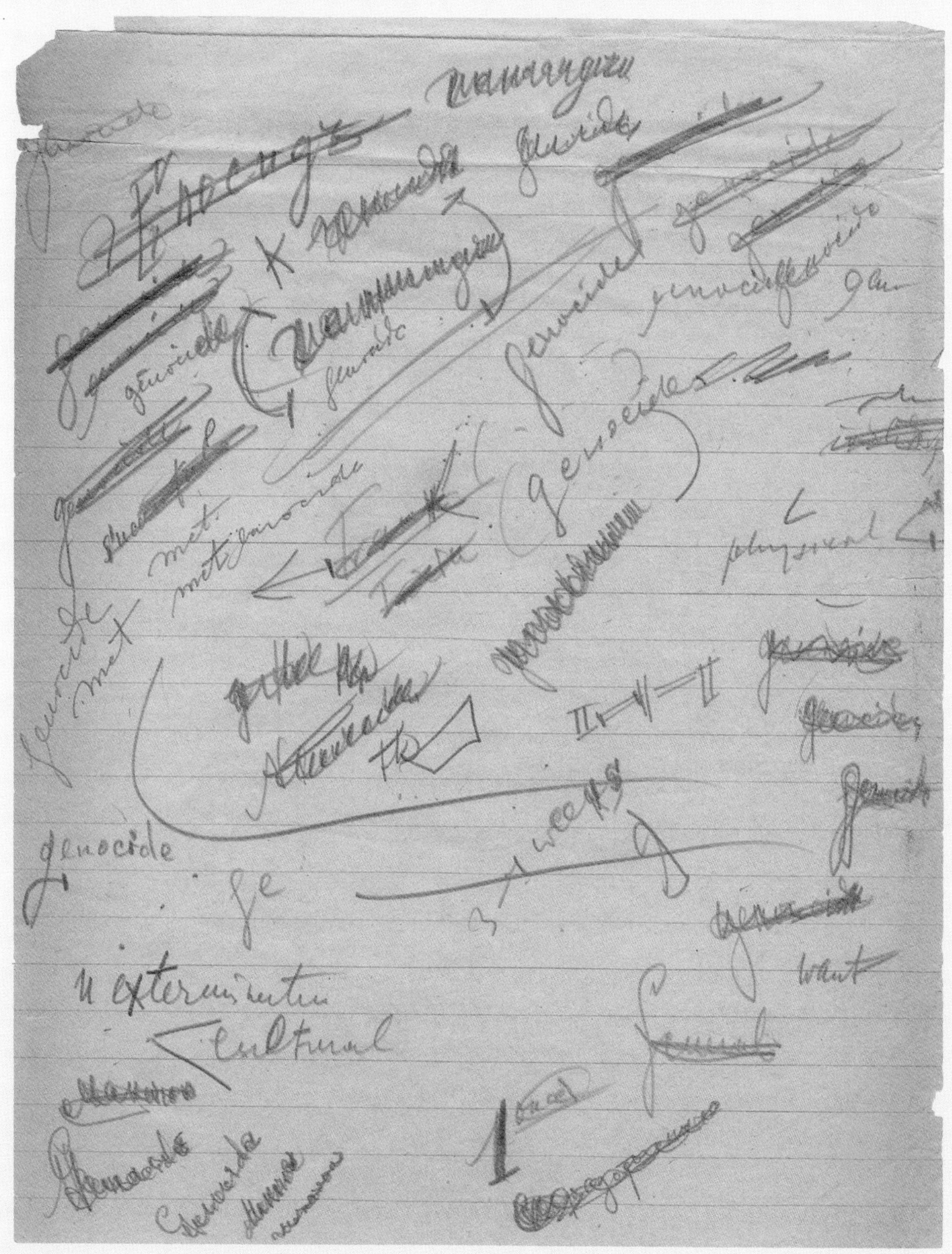
genocide
physical
Cultural
want

Second World War was swiftly followed by the Cold War, which rendered the sort of collaboration across nations that had made the IMT viable completely impossible. Throughout the period, international law remained in a state of suspended animation in practical terms.

In the end, it was not global conflicts between nations but regional wars where international law reasserted itself. The world was sufficiently horrified by the violence that erupted in two separate conflicts in the 1990s to remobilise systems of transnational justice in response. In the former Yugoslavia, declarations of independence by four of the federal state's six republics led to a vicious internecine war. Among a series of terrible incidents targeting civilians, which included ethnic cleansing and the besieging of towns and cities, the mass execution of Bosnian Muslim men and boys by the Bosnian Serb Army in Srebrenica in July 1995 would become a defining event. It would ultimately be recognised by the International Court of Justice as the first designated genocide in Europe since the Second World War. In Rwanda the mass murder of 800,000 Tsutsi and moderate Hutus by Hutu extremists acting for the government was also similarly recognised.

Ad hoc tribunals were established by the UN to assemble prosecution cases against those responsible for these crimes. These were known as the ICTY and ICTR respectively. Unlike Nuremberg, both these tribunals included previous heads of government among the defendants. At the ICTR, former interim Prime Minister Jean Kambanda was charged, while at the ICTY the former president of Serbia, Slobodan Milošević, was charged, as well as the former president of Republika Srpska, Radovan Karadžić.

The ICTY became the first trial to charge individuals with the crime of genocide, in the cases of Ratko Mladić and Radovan Karadžić, on 25 July 1995. The ICTR became the first to secure convictions for the crime, when Jean-Paul Akayesu – the former mayor of Taba commune – was found guilty on 2 September 1998.

As international law evolved across the course of the twentieth century, four core crimes emerged: war crimes, crimes against humanity, genocide and crimes of aggression. An important development in these laws since Nuremberg

Graves are dug during a Bosnian Muslim mass funeral in the Lions Cemetery in Sarajevo, June 1992. During the siege of the city, which lasted for 1,425 days, nearly 5,500 civilians were killed alongside around 5,000 soldiers.

Médecins Sans Frontières aid workers collect Rwandan dead from the roadside at a Hutu refugee camp near Goma, Zaire, August 1994. Across around 100 days, over 800,000 Tstusi, together with some moderate Hutu and Twa, were massacred by Hutu extremists.

SLAVICA
JANKOVIĆ
1956-1992
VERA

DAIHATS

– reflected in the charges brought at the ICTY and the ICTR – was the recognition of rape and sexual violence as chargeable offences in the context of war crimes, crimes against humanity and genocide. While there was awareness of the existence of such criminal behaviour before the IMT, there was never any effort to register its specificity. By the 1990s, there was an avowed resolution to ensure that it was properly acknowledged.

Though international law is now established, there is considerable uncertainty about which direction it will take in the years to come. Its effectiveness relies on the agreement and commitment of all nations, and this is not easy to secure – least of all during periods of geopolitical tension. Since Nuremberg, those prosecuted in international criminal courts have either been involved in civil wars or from countries within Africa. Thus the resolve of those in the West to stand in judgement of their allies has never been properly tested. Nor has the willingness of the world's most powerful nations to yield to the authority of an international court. It remains to be seen whether the system, as it exists, can withstand that pressure.

It is also likely that the four core crimes will need to be amended, or changed, in future. Genocide is an offence that is very difficult to prosecute as it is currently conceived, and there are some who believe it causes more problems than it solves as an instrument of law. Its status is bolstered, in part, by the fact that it is underpinned by a specific international convention. No similar convention currently exists for crimes against humanity, though it is likely that one will eventually emerge. In recent years, discussions about the addition of 'ecocide' as a fifth crime have gained momentum in response to growing concerns about climate change. While it is eminently possible that this new law will be formalised, it will likely take some time.

Whatever the course of international law in the future, one thing is clear: its origin will always be tied to the events that unfolded at the Palace of Justice in Nuremberg, between November 1945 and October 1946. It was not the building that determined this historic occurrence, nor the city itself, whose name now dominates the memory of the trial, but a small group of lawyers united by conviction and common purpose, who made it happen.

A sketch for *The Nuremberg Trial* by Laura Knight.

Notes

Chapter One

1. 'Nazi Crimes in Poland: Allied Protest to the World: Destroying Lives and Culture', 'destroying not only the lives and property, but also the culture and religious existence of the defenceless population...In addition to the persecution of the Poles there is the atrocious treatment inflicted on the members of the Jewish community...They reaffirm the responsibility of Germany for these crimes and their determination to right the wrongs thus inflicted on the Polish people.' 'Nazi Crimes in Poland: Allied Protest to the World: Destroying Lives and Culture', *Western Morning News*, 18 April 1940, p.5 © *Western Morning News* During the Parliamentary debate on 17 December 1942, Viscount Samuel suggested, 'that the present Nazi atrocities against the Jews were on a far vaster scale than the Armenian massacres of fifty years ago...' 'Planned Cruelty: Armenian Massacres Only Remotely Parallel, says Lord Samuel', *The Scotsman*, 18 December 1942, p. 5 © *The Scotsman*
2. 'French Nation's Protest Day: A War Aim', *Newcastle Journal*, 27 October 1941, p.1 © *Newcastle Journal*
3. 'Atrocities To Jews: The United Nations Pledge Retribution: Ring-Leaders and Underlings to be Treated Alike: Massacred in Mass Executions', *The Scotsman*, 18 December 1942, p.5 © *The Scotsman*
4. 'A Bestial Policy: Persecutors of Jews Not to Escape: United Nations Declaration', *Liverpool Daily Post*, 18 December 1942, p. 3 © *Liverpool Daily Post*
5. 'Moscow Declaration Of Allies' War and Peace Aims', *The Civil and Military Gazette* (Lahore), 3 November 1943, p.6 © *The Civil and Military Gazette*
6. Ibid
7. Ibid
8. 'Death for Hitler' by Professor Berriedale Keith, *Leicester Evening Mail*, 11 December 1943, p.3 © *Leicester Evening Mail*
9. The 1943 Krasnodar trial was the first open military tribunal to take place during the war. Eleven Soviet citizens accused of betraying their country and collaborating with the Nazis were found guilty; eight were hanged in front of tens of thousands of cheering Soviet citizens.
10. The war crimes trial in Lublin convicted six Germans of murder at Dachau and Oranienburg concentration camps. This was followed by the Majdanek trial.
11. Bradley F Smith, *Reaching Judgment at Nuremberg* (New York: HarperCollins, 1977), pp. 36–37 © HarperCollins
12. Ibid
13. Jeremy Hicks, *First Films of the Holocaust: Soviet Cinema and the Genocide of the Jews, 1938-1946* (Pittsburgh, University of Pittsburgh Press, 2012), pp. 186–187
14. Smith, p.29
15. Ibid, p.42
16. Ibid, p.63
17. *Western Morning News*, 2 November 1945, p. 5
18. 'Nuremberg Trial Opens: Twenty Nazis Face Accusers: Judge on Unique Trial', *The Liverpool Echo*, 20 November 1945, p.6 © *The Liverpool Echo*
19. 'Red-Letter Trial', *Hartlepool Northern Daily Mail*, 21 November 1945, p.3 © *Hartlepool Northern Daily Mail*

Chapter Two

1. Private Papers of G D Roberts QC OBE (Documents.11599) © Rights Holder
2. Private Papers of K G Burton (Documents.20930) © Rights Holder

Chapter Three

1. Interview with Peter John Ambrose Calvocoressi © IWM (13282)
2. Ibid
3. Private Papers of Dr R Thompson (Documents.13176) © Rights Holder
4. Ibid
5. Reports on Nuremberg Trials Prisoner's Procedures © Crown. IWM (Documents.10214)
6. Report on Suicide of Dr Robert Ley / Headquarters / 6850th Internal Security Detachment / International Military Tribunal / APO 403 U.S. Army © Courtesy of Cornell University Law Library, Donovan Nuremberg Trials Collection
7. Reports on Nuremberg Trials Prisoner's Procedures © Crown. IWM (Documents.10214)
8. Roberts (Documents.11599)

Chapter Four

1. Roberts (Documents.11599)
2. Private Papers of Colonel H D Turrall (Documents.6371) © Rights Holder
3. Ibid
4 Roberts (Documents.11599)
5. Private Papers of Lieutenant Colonel A M Man DSO OBE © IWM (Documents.4482)
6. Calvocoressi © IWM (13282)
7. Whitney Harris, *Tyranny on Trial: The Evidence at Nuremberg* (New York: Barnes and Noble, 1995), xxxv–xxxvi © Texas A&M University Press
8. Alexandra Zapruder (ed.), *Salvaged Pages: Young Writers' Diaries of the Holocaust* (New Haven: Yale University Press, 2002) p. 412 © Yale University Press
9. Personal account of attendance at Nuremberg Trials (Documents.26447) © Rights Holder
10. Calvocoressi (20824)

Chapter Five

1. *Gloucester Echo*, 17 September 1945, p.4 © *Gloucester Echo*
2. Ibid
3. Interview with Julius Stafford-Baker (5398, Reel 3) © IWM (5398)
4. 'Greatest Trial in History: 20 Nazis Face Court To-Day', *Liverpool Daily Post*, 20 November 1945, p.1 © *Liverpool Daily Post*
5. *Belfast News Letter*, 20 October 1945, p.3 © *Belfast News Letter*
6. *Aberdeen Press and Journal*, 21 May 1946, p.2 © *Aberdeen Press and Journal*
7. It was reported that the German press had 10 seats and the British 35. *Shields Daily News*, 28 September 1946, p.8. © *Shields Daily News*
8. *Belfast News Letter*, 21 November 1945, p.5 © *Belfast News Letter*
9. *Birmingham Gazette*, 17 January 1946 © *Birmingham Gazette*
10. Donald Bloxham, *Genocide on Trial: War Crimes Trials and the formation of Holocaust History and Memory*, (Oxford: Oxford University Press, 2001) pp.101–109
11. TNA WO219/5108, HQ OSS, War Crimes Photographic Project, 9 June 1945
12. Jean-Christophe Klotz, directors, *Filmmakers for the Prosecution* (2022), produced by Sandra Schulberg, Céline Nusse and Paul Rozenberg
13. Hoffman was also the father-in-law of IMT defendant Baldur von Schirach and personal friend of Hitler.
14. Memorandum to the Planning Committee, from Commander James B Donovan, Visual Presentation: i. Motion Picture Evidence, A. General Plan, 19 November 1945, p.5. © Courtesy of Cornell University Law Library, Donovan Nuremberg Trials Collection
15. 'MOI thanks Stirling Man', *Stirling Observer*, 9 October 1945, p.3 © *Stirling Observer*
16. The Avalon Project, Nuremberg Trial Proceedings, Volume 2, Eighth Day, Thursday 29 November 1945, Mr J T Dodd, p.430
17. The Avalon Project, Nuremberg Trial Proceedings, Volume 2, Third Day, Wednesday 21 November 1945, Mr Justice Jackson, p.101
18. Roberts (Documents.11599)
19. This took place on 8 November 1945, see Sandra Schulberg, *Filmmakers for the Prosecution: The Making of Nuremberg: Its Lesson for Today*, p.13
20. The Avalon Project, Nuremberg Trial Proceedings, Volume 3, Nineteenth Day, Thursday 13 December 1945, p.535

Chapter Six

1. The Private Papers of Ian McIlwraith © Rights Holder
2. David Low, *Low's Autobiography*, (London: Michael Joseph, 1956), p.358 © Rights Holder
3. Ibid, p.360
4. Ibid, p.361
5. Ibid, p.359
6. Low, p. 359
7. Low, p.360
8. Interview with Hedy Epstein (12397, Reel 6) © IWM (12397)
9. Interview with Joseph Otto Flatter (4765, reel 1) © IWM (4765)
10. Ibid
11. Flatter (4765, reel 2)
12. Ibid

13. Barbara C Morden, *Laura Knight: A Life* (Carmarthen: McNidder and Grace, 2021) p. 230 © McNidder and Grace
14. Ibid
15. Ibid
16. *The Press and Journal*, 4 May 1946, p.4 © *The Press and Journal*
17. 'Dame Laura Knight's Nuremberg Painting', *Nottingham Evening Post*, 20 April 1946, p.1 © *Nottingham Evening Post*
18. Laura Knight, *The Magic of a Line: The Autobiography of Laura Knight* (London: William Kimber and Co., 1965) p. 295 © The Trustees of the Estate of Dame Laura Knight DBE RA RWS
19. Ibid
20. Ibid

Chapter Seven

1. The Seventeenth Organisation Meeting of the International Military Tribunal, 29 October 1945, convened for the purpose of developing criminal procedures
2. *The Saturday Evening Post* © *The Saturday Evening Post*

Chapter Eight

1. Interview with Peter Uiberall (12054, reel 4) © IWM (12054)
2. Ibid
3. Ibid
4. Ibid
5. Airey Neave, Nuremberg: *A Personal Record of the Trial of the Major Nazi War Criminals* (Hull: Biteback Publishing, 2021) p. 253 © Airey Neave, reprinted by permission of Biteback Publishing
6. Ibid
7. Interview with Seaghan Maynes (12065) © IWM (12065)
8. 'Speeding Trial at Nuremberg', *Western Morning News*, 6 February 1946, p.3 © *Western Morning News*
9. Benjamin B Ferencz, in a video interview filmed on 15 April 2010, as an extra to the disc release of *Nuremberg: Its Lesson for Today* (2014). Ferenz was one of the prosecutors on the 12 subsequent trials to the IMT, the Nuremberg Military Tribunals
10. Denis Martin, 'Nazis Smirk as Judge Curbs the U.S.' Prosecutor', *Daily Herald*, 19 December 1945, p. 4 © *Daily Herald*
11. Ibid
12. Aubrey Hammond, 'Goering Cut Short by Judge: Laughter in Court', *Newcastle Journal*, 22 November 1945, p.1 © *Newcastle Journal*
13. Major William Walsh, IMT Proceedings, 14 December 1945, p.572
14. Denis Martin, 'Horror Film Turned Nuremberg Gang Pale: Two of Them Jib', *Daily Herald*, 30 November 1945, p.4 © *Daily Herald*
15. Aubrey Hammond, 'Schacht Turned Eyes From Horror Film', *Daily Despatch*, 30 November 1945, p.1 © *Daily Despatch*
16. Ronald Clark, 'British United Press, Nazi Chiefs See Horror Film', *Yorkshire Post and Leeds Intelligencer*, 30 November 1945, p.1 © *Yorkshire Post and Leeds Intelligencer*
17. Denis Martin, 'Nazis Smirk as Judge Curbs the U.S.' Prosecutor', *Daily Herald*, 19 December 1945, © *Daily Herald*
18. Interview with George Vassiltchikov (10938) © IWM (10938)
19. Calvocoressi (13282, reel 1) © IWM (13282)
20. Neave, p.247–8
21. 'Nuremberg Film Show of "Nazi Plan": Accused in Scenes of Their Heyday', *The Coventry Evening Telegraph*, 11 December 1945, p.1 © *The Coventry Evening Telegraph*
22. Ibid
23. Bernard Murphy, 'Nuremberg Film Excites Goering: Hitler Gang See Themselves Strut and Heil', *Lancashire Evening Post*, 11 December 1945, p.1 © *Lancashire Evening Post*
24. Ray Kellogg and George Stevens, directors, *The Nazi Plan* (1945), United States Counsel for the Prosecution of Axis Criminality; Twentieth Century Fox Film Corporation
25. Joseph E Persico, *Nuremberg: Infamy on Trial* (New York: Penguin, 1995) p.159 © Rights Holder
26. 'Woman's Story of Horror Camps', *Edinburgh Evening News*, 28 January 1946, p.3 © *Edinburgh Evening News*

27. 'Nuremberg Horror Story', *Lancashire Evening Post*, 28 January 1946, p.1 © *Lancashire Evening Post*
28. 'Live Babies Thrown in Furnace', AP and Reuter, *Birmingham Daily Gazette*, 29 January 1946, p.4 © *Birmingham Daily Gazette*
29. 'Branded Woman Tells of Torture', *Daily Herald*, 29 January 1946, p. 5 © *Daily Herald*
30. Uiberall (12054, reel 4) © IWM (12054)
31. Ibid
32. Neave, p.288–289
33. Bernard Murphy, *Lancashire Evening Post*, 22 March 1946, p.1 © *Lancashire Evening Post*
34. These statements were recorded by Trial psychologist Dr Gustave Gilbert in the prisoners' cells on 1 October 1946. See Gustave Gilbert, *The Nuremberg Diary* (Cambridge: Da Capo Press, 1995), pp. 393–395
35. 'Nuremberg Wives Say Goodbye: Judgment Day', *The Sunday Post*, 29 September 1946, p.1 © *The Sunday Post*
36. *Edinburgh Evening News*, 30 September 1946, p.3 © *Edinburgh Evening News*
37. Persico, p.420
38. Kerr MacFee, *Gloucester Citizen*, 17 October 1946, p.6 © *Gloucester Citizen*
39. 'Comment on Drama of Nuremberg: Branded A "Coward"', *Belfast News Letter*, 17 October 1946, p.3 © *Belfast News Letter*
40. Ibid
41. Maynes (12065)
42. Gault MacGowan, *New York Sun* © *New York Sun*
43. 'Goering Feared He Would be Strangled', *Aberdeen Press and Journal*, 25 October 1946, p.1 © *Aberdeen Press and Journal*

Chapter Nine

1. Interview with Michael Etkind (10406, reel 22) © IWM (10406)
2. Ibid
3. Interview with Elfriede Lawrence (17511) © IWM (17511)
4. *Sunday Dispatch*, 2 December 1945, p.4 © *Sunday Dispatch*
5. Christian Delage, *La Vérité par l'image: De Nuremberg au Procès Milosevic* (Paris: Denoël, 2006) p.251
6. United Nations International Residual Mechanism for Criminal Tribunals. The Prosecution's Evidence Collection (2025) irmct.org.uk/specials/prosecution-evidence-collection/en/
7. International Committee of the Red Cross. *Charter of the Nuremberg Tribunal: Article 6(b)* (1945) IHL Treaties Database. ihl-databases.icrc.org/en/ihl-treaties/nuremberg-tribunal-charter-1945/article-6b

List of Illustrations

All images are IWM © unless otherwise stated

Chapter One
BU 4006, [Photograph Number: 16775] © United States Holocaust Memorial Museum, WPN 132, National Archives (111-SC-252946), Charles Alexander US Chief of Counsel for the Prosecution of Axis Criminality. Harry S Truman Library & Museum (72-818)

Chapter Two
MH 11470, HU 44924, G39HJT © Alamy, HU 93589, Charles Alexander US Chief of Counsel for the Prosecution of Axis Criminality. Harry S Truman Library & Museum (72-853), Documents.25704/A, Documents.11599/A, Charles Alexander US Chief of Counsel for the Prosecution of Axis Criminality. Harry S Truman Library & Museum (72-829), Documents.20930

Chapter Three
Art.IWM ART LD 5591, CXW567 © Alamy, HU 40217, HU 7253, HU 7219, 2J2JGH9 © Alamy, DEU 503409, MH 6041, FOY 3, EA 65715, CPMPX3 © Alamy, GER 1260, D5K43A © Alamy, MH 1093, C45P12 © Alamy, [78579] © United States Holocaust Memorial Museum, A 14906, MH 608, FOY 3, HU 7234, BY8TBP © Alamy, D88MX9 © Alamy, BU 5539, BU 6713, FLM 153, [80641] © United States Holocaust Memorial Museum, BU 6715, Documents.13176, Documents.10214/A, Documents.10214/D, BU 6703, DEU 503578

Chapter Four
Charles Alexander US Chief of Counsel for the Prosecution of Axis Criminality. Harry S Truman Library & Museum (72-867), HU 97316, Documents.27373, Documents.11599, Documents.27373, DB3RY3 © Alamy, National Archives (111-SC-216346 - Album 5568), Art.IWM ART LD 5863, HU 87403, Documents.27373/A, [RG-60.2842] © United States Holocaust Memorial Museum

Chapter Five
HU 65519, HU 66138, HU 60981, HU 093592, © Rights Holder (Art.ILN: 2386), FOY 3_02, MGH 114_01, MGH 113_02, Art.IWM ART LD 5726, MGH 113_01, MGH 113_02

Chapter Six
Art.IWM ART LD 5930, © Rights Holder (Art.ILN: 2304), © Rights Holder (Art.IWM ART 17451 12), ©Rights Holder (Art.ILN: 2303), Art.IWM ART 16351, Art.IWM ART LD 6862, Art.IWM ART LD 5866, Art.IWM ART LD 5725, Art.IWM ART LD 5724, Art.IWM ART LD 5723, Art.IWM ART LD 5862, Art.IWM ART LD 5798

Chapter Seven
2R76Y0R © Alamy, HU 60979, HU 60978, Art.IWM ART 17028

Chapter Eight
Art.IWM ART LD 5865, MH 30457, HU 62728, HU 26596, MH 24088, AP 286849, HU 71699, NWT 28, Art.IWM ART LD 5864, Art. IWM ART LD 5929, BU 13196

Chapter Nine
© Rights Holder (5.3.6_Totem_HL4 taking silk 1959), 'Writings: Notes, handwritten, undated', Box 5, Raphael Lemkin Papers, Rare Book & Manuscript Library, Columbia University, BOS 212, CT 1656, Art.IWM ART LD 5928

About the Authors

Dr James Bulgin is Head of Public History at IWM and was previously Head of Content for the award-winning Holocaust Galleries. He is an expert on modern European history, and particularly the Holocaust and the nuclear threat during the Cold War. He is the author of *The Holocaust* and co-author of *The New Holocaust Galleries at the Imperial War Museum London: Conception, Design, Interpretation* (DeGruyter). James has spoken at a range of international conferences, has written for *The Guardian, BBC History Magazine* and *The Radio Times*, and regularly appears in the media discussing twentieth-century conflict. He is the presenter of *How the Holocaust Began* (BBC) and has appeared as an onscreen expert on programmes including *D-Day The Unheard Tapes, Rise of the Nazis* (for which he is also a historical advisor) and *Secrets of the Imperial War Museum*. He was historical consultant for the Sam Mendes film *What They Found* and will shortly be seen in major new upcoming series for Channel 4 and the History Channel.

Dr Toby Haggith is a Senior Curator in the Department of Second World War and Mid-Twentieth-Century Conflict at IWM. He was, for ten years, the programmer of the Museum's public cinema and conceived and ran the IWM Student Film Festival (now the IWM Short Film Festival). In recent years, he has been closely involved with film restoration, notably on *The Battle of the Somme* (1916), *The Battle of the Ancre* (1917) and *Battle of Arras* (1917). He was the director of the restoration and completion of *German Concentration Camps Factual Survey* (1945/2014) and oversaw the production of the Blu-ray/DVD version, which won an award at the 2018 Bologna Ritrovato DVD awards. He has published various essays on film and history and is the co-editor with Joanna Newman of *Holocaust and the Moving Image: Film and Television Representations Since 1933* (London: 2005). In 2006, while selecting films for a cinema programme to mark the anniversary of the Nuremberg trial, he came across a film in the IWM collection titled, 'Composite Material of Belsen Atrocities: Film used as evidence for Judge Advocate General during Nuremberg trials', but which he suspected was the long-forgotten British film screened as evidence at the Belsen trial on 20 September 1945. After extensive research he was able to confirm this film as the *Belsen Camp Evidence Film* (discussed in this book) and is currently completing an in-depth study exploring the use of film at the Belsen trial in the context of British evidence filming during the Second World War.

Acknowledgements

James would like to thank Lara Bateman, Sarah Newman, David Fenton, Georgia Davies, James Taylor, Anthony Richards, Dr Robert Sherwood, Professor Kenneth Morrison and Hannah Llewellyn-Jones for their integral contributions to *Nuremberg* – and Menachem Z Rosensaft, Philippe Joseph Sands KC FRSL Hon FBA and John and Ann Tusa for their input and advice on the subject in the years prior.

Toby would like to thank Sarah Holdaway for her comments on chapter six, and for arranging a research visit to the Feliks Topolski archive. Toby would also like to thank Claire Kessie for her comments on earlier drafts of his chapters.

Index

Note: Page numbers in italics refer to images; those followed by 'n' to the endnotes.